INSIDE THAI SOCIETY
RELIGION • EVERYDAY LIFE • CHANGE

NIELS MULDER

SILKWORM BOOKS

Other titles by Niels Mulder:

Inside Southeast Asia: Religion • Everyday Life • Cultural Change
Inside Indonesian Society: Cultural Change in Java
Thai Images: The Culture of the Public World
Filipino Images: Culture of the Public Word

ISBN 974-7551-24-1

This edition is first published by Silkworm Books in 2000, reprint in 2001.

Silkworm Books
104/5 Chiang Mai-Hot Road, M. 7, Suthep, Muang, Chiang Mai 50200, Thailand
E-mail address: silkworm@loxinfo.co.th

Typeset by Silk Type
Cover design by Umaphon Soetphannuk
Printed in Thailand by O. S. Printing House, Bangkok

01 02 03 04 05   6 5 4 3 2

CONTENTS

PREFACE

For more than thirty-five years I have been interested in Thailand. When I went there for the first time, in 1965, I studied the language, Buddhism, and the involvement of monks in community development. These early experiences resulted in a modest monograph in which I explored the presumed relationship between religion and economic action. In the 1960s, such assumptions were ordinary fare. In many of the anthropological publications of those days, we find, as a matter of course, assertions that the Thais act, think, or behave in certain ways because they are Buddhists.

During my early research, I soon found out that there is much truth in the idea that to be a Thai is to be a Buddhist, but what I had still to discover was what that meant. It became almost immediately apparent that self-styled orthodox reformers and outsiders' ideas about Buddhism were a poor guide to understand Thai behaviour and mentality. What I had to explore was the view from within.

After staying—intermittently—three years in Bangkok and, later, another three in Chiang Mai, I finally published my first attempt at understanding the logic of Thai behaviour, at least as I observed it in the urban, most often middle-class setting. This study was produced by Editions Duang Kamol as *Everyday Life in Thailand: An Interpretation*. The book was variously reviewed, by foreigners, as insightful, scholarly and entertaining, important, theoretically powerful, and recommended as 'a valuable handbook for all who wish to have a better understanding of Thai behaviour'.

On its way to becoming a 'classic' text, the original book was repeatedly edited, revised, and updated; new chapters were added, others deleted. The title also changed. From 1990 onwards, it became known as *Inside Thai Society*, of which two editions appeared with Duang Kamol and one with

The Pepin Press. The idea behind the present Silkworm Books edition is to make the interpretation of Thai action, for which the book became well-known, available to a wide public. Changes to the previous version are mainly editorial, and no attempt has been made to keep abreast of the political scene in the capital where, in spite of rapidly revolving political fortunes, the ways in which power is wielded remain substantially the same. While the main title has been maintained, the publication's academic subtitle has been reduced to three snippets that rather accurately reflect what the reader may expect to find information about.

Despite the many revisions, four original chapters, of the seven of the first edition, are still recognizably present. These are the two chapters on religion and the two that interpret everyday action. Meanwhile the book has expanded to ten chapters, three of which deal explicitly with change and the arising of middle-class culture.

The latter topic, namely how modern urbanites are likely to perceive and to discuss contemporary society, is the subject of *Thai Images: The Culture of the Public World* (Silkworm Books, 1997). In order to understand how the public world is constructed and animated, it is still very useful to familiarize oneself with the basic perceptions analyzed in the present volume. After all, however much the appearance of things has changed, and however many entirely new phenomena have come to the fore, we can also witness numerous cultural continuities, in education, religion, family ideology, and in the ways power is wielded.

These continuities have, of course, to be traced through a scene in change. Rapid urbanization and a changing economy have resulted in the rise of middle classes. The locus of power, formerly with the military and bureaucracy, has shifted to businessmen-politicians. On the religious stage, new sects and cults, controversies, and a formidable trade in amulets have arisen. Money has become extraordinarily important in social life. Even so, after all these thirty-five years, Thailand still feels very much the same, and not only because of its delicious food. There is continuity in change, as with this book, that may be helpful to newcomers in finding their bearings.

Niels Mulder
Chiang Mai 1999

NOTE ON SPELLING AND THE USE OF THAI WORDS AND NAMES

Generally, Thai words have been transliterated in accordance with the system developed by the Royal Institute, excepting, some familiar and time-honoured romanizations of common Thai terms and names, as well as some internationally common Sanskrit and Pali words. Names have been spelled according to the preferences, when known, of the people concerned.

INTRODUCTION

Thailand is often called The Land of Smiles, a sobriquet which sounds at once pleasant and mysterious. At the same time that a smile may suggest good humour, it is one of the most enigmatic of expressions as well. A smile may be a sign of kindness, of forgiveness, or friendly inclinations; a smile may also be merely polite, a way to smooth interaction or a sign that one is willing to listen. A smile may indicate agreement, or self-confidence, but may also be a means to gently express one's opposition or doubt. A person on the defensive may smile, and one may smile when sad, or hurt, or even insulted. It has been said that the Thais have a smile for every emotion, and with so many nuances of smiling, the smile often hides more than it reveals.

This book aims to look behind smiles and appearances to discover some of the basic ideas that give meaning and structure to life in Thai society. However confusing the practice of everyday life may appear to the outside observer, the participants themselves seem to take it for granted and to know their way; to them, the conduct of their lives appears predictable, embedded as it is in the shared expectations that lend regularity to social life.

In other words, with this book we primarily aim at discovering those regularities and expectations that pervade everyday life. We shall see that smiles and appearances are an important part of it, and we shall investigate why that is so and what it means—or may mean—to the participants concerned. We shall delve into the content of relationships, assess their quality and sort them out, because, depending on why and to whom one relates, bonds will have different meanings and shapes.

It will become apparent that religion, or rather religious practice and conceptualization, is an extraordinarily fertile field to dig for basic ideas that seem to recur in everyday life. Whatever the official tenets of a great faith may be, it is almost a universal rule that religious practice is cast into the mould of a local society whose styles and ways it will reflect.

Because of this anthropological insight, religion and everyday life will be described primarily as practice. Through baring the basic regularities, we shall then be able to reach certain more theoretical statements about Thai behaviour and society. These are the type of statements a sociologist will call a 'theory of action', with which we mean that presumed actors' motivations and expectations are part of the explanations. Because of this attempt to grasp the subjective element of action, the book is named *Inside Thai Society*.

This society is, like any other, always in flux. Over the past thirty or forty years, the pace of change has accelerated, and particularly the process of social differentiation seems to be occurring at high speed. Because of this, the study pays considerable attention to what is apparently new in Thai society, while demonstrating that certain basic ideas and practices pervade the changing practice of life.

Chapter by chapter

Chapter 1 presents us first with an overview of the process of economic and socio-cultural change that leads to an increasingly diversifying society. Over the past century and a half, Thai society has opened up to the world of global ideas that compete with local perceptions. The tensions between these various ideas and the gradual changes in the dominant world view are part of an irreversible movement that seems to be characterized more by a continuity-in-change than by abrupt discontinuities. This is also apparent in the sluggish development of a modern political culture that is considered in the second section of the chapter.

Chapter 2 may be considered as the backbone of this work. It contains an analysis of two important basic ideas such as they reveal themselves in religious, and to a certain extent secular, practice. It is the ideas of Power and Goodness. These ideas are no antipodes. In practice, they mix. Depending on their mixture, they allow for the classification of social behaviour and supernatural phenomena on a scale that ranges from serenity and wisdom to total unreliability and chaos, from Nirvana to pure hell.

Thinking in those extremes, however, is not very practical, and neither allows us to understand everyday life nor religious practice. Besides, goodness in itself is thought to be powerful: it has the power to overcome evil and chaos. And when insulted, it triggers off bad karma and revenge. What these riddles can reveal will be unravelled in this second chapter.

Chapters 3 and 4 explore the perceptions and attitudes that inform Thai behaviour. The subject is approached by taking issue with the interpretations of other social scientists, dating from a period in which Thai behaviour was widely held to be unpredictable to the extreme. This presumed irregularity melts away in the face of rather ordinary sociological analysis in terms of relative social distance, the hierarchy in which relationships occur, familiarity versus awe, and suchlike. The participants' perceptions so structured are reinforced by the parallel perceptions of goodness and power. Social characteristics, such as power, status and prestige, are readily seen through the lens the perception of Power provides, whereas elements like trust, life-cycle status, and inhibition can best be understood through a reflection on Goodness. The fact that these classifications are not just an academic fabrication can be amply illustrated by the indigenous valuation of certain practical roles that are thought to exemplify the basic ideas of Power and Goodness. Of course, all behaviour and interaction cannot be understood in these terms. It is, therefore, also necessary to consider individual choice, reserve, and relaxation as the counterpoints of 'regular' comportment.

Chapter 5 explores the ideological fog that hides the realities of life in the urban middle-class family from critical observation. Often the subject of family life seems to be taboo and beyond discussion. This reinforces the tendency to idealize certain roles, especially the one of 'mother' as representing reliability and goodness, in contrast with the irresponsible male standing for amoral power. As such, the chapter is a consideration of the Thai gender ideology that still acts as a powerful conservative force.

Chapter 6 explores the views on social life of various novelists. These authors definitely do not write with the purpose of informing foreign anthropologists, but rather want to open the eyes of their readership for the stark realities of their society. As a result, they provide independent points of observation that are prejudiced according to their personal perceptions, but that have not been influenced by the outsider researcher. Because of this, they afford original images that can then be used to test the usefulness of the interpretations that have been developed earlier on in this work. These interpretations are summarized in chapter 7.

Chapter 8 is a discussion of the most ubiquitous of Thai institutions, namely Buddhism, and its part in creating a national identity. The chapter also devotes some thought to the animistic understanding of religion in the course of a discussion of Buddhist reform movements, and explores ideas about education and knowledge.

Chapter 9 considers the question of how people learn to think about the public world of nation, state, and wider society. It concentrates on the ideology of 'the system of democratic government headed by the King' as it is presented in officially authorized textbooks currently used in elementary school. This analysis concurs with the prevailing perception of society in moralistic instead of sociological, or structural, terms. This point of view has its repercussions for the understanding of democracy and human rights discussed in chapter 10. Through focusing on the indigenous image of the external world, the transformations of the ideas of democracy and human rights, and their adaptation to Thai political practice, become clear. Altogether, these last two chapters cast a stark light on the social imagination of the new urban middle classes. Finally, the conclusion reconsiders some of the interpretations developed in the course of this study.

THE THAI OPENING UP TO THE WORLD

The development of culture, of the ideas people live with, is a steady process, always on the move, and to begin its story from a certain date is arbitrary indeed. But given that the gradual opening up of society to modernity is a crucial theme in explaining current cultural development in Thailand, then the choice of 1855 seems reasonably appropriate. In that year, the Bowring Treaty, which did away with the royal monopolies and opened the country up to foreign trade, was concluded.

King Mongkut, the fourth monarch of the current dynasty, with whom it was negotiated, also exemplifies the trend towards the opening up of the country to foreign ideas. He learned English, held discourses with foreign missionaries on religious subjects, and was interested in science and systematic observation. It was even these latter passions that caused his untimely demise due to malaria caught during a journey to the south to observe a solar eclipse in 1868.

So, while the Bowring Treaty stands at the beginning of Thailand's gradual involvement in the world economic system, it also signals the entry into participation in the world-wide circulation of ideas, of a dawning awareness of events going on elsewhere in the world, and of the first devising of strategies to cope with global political developments, above all the encroachment of the European colonial powers in Southeast Asia. All this comes clearly into focus during the reign of Mongkut's successor, King Chulalongkorn.

When the young heir came to the throne, the country was still basically feudal in its political organization, with local grandees exercising considerable control of the kingdom's peripheral regions. This nobility lorded it over a peasant population that was liable to corvée (statute labour), and in itself divided into freeman and slave classes. Naturally, this aristocracy had no interest in supporting a strong central authority, or the administrative reorganization of the realm.

King Chulalongkorn was a purposeful man who understood the demands of his time, yet it wasn't until 1892 that he finally succeeded in overruling the feudal elite's attempts to block his schemes, thus opening the way for administrative reforms, systematic modernization, and absolute royal control. From this time onwards, a salaried, Bangkok-appointed bureaucracy was instituted, control over the Buddhist monkhood *(Sangha)* established, general education introduced, and a modern communications network built up. In the process, the corvée system was abandoned and the slaves emancipated (Prizzia, 1986).

Inspiration for all this was sought in the administrative models of the powerful colonial states of the region, in modern forms of organization, and in western education. To direct the reforms and advance the country's development, men were needed with modern training, also necessitating the sending abroad of bright young students of common descent. It was these latter foreign-educated commoners in the army and bureaucracy who brought to an end the rather short-lived period of royal absolutism and inaugurated the period of constitutional monarchy in 1932.

So, from the 1850s onwards, we witness a gradual expansion of the economy, with the export of rice becoming the mainstay (Ingram, 1971), along with the immigration of vast numbers of Chinese labourers to build the railways, new canals and other elements of the modern infrastructure, and also to work in the southern tin mines, which increased their output dramatically at this time as well. All of this contributed to the vast changes that were taking place in the thoughts and belief patterns of a significant segment of the urban population. From the acceptance of a hierarchical, feudal order as a naturally given law of society—an idea that can still be encountered among members of the old nobility, and among rural folks in remote areas—a new perception was evolving in urban circles during the period of administrative modernization that introduced the alien concept of nationalism, taking Europe as the source of inspiration. This ferment of new ideas, followed through logically, then led on to the questioning of the legitimacy of absolute royal rights and privileges.

Equipped with such European concepts as socialism, democracy, and constitutionalism, the new men at the helm not only held ideas that are often still a little out of place in Thai society, but also promoted them at the newly established Thammasat University that, then as now, is the bastion of modern social thought. At the same time, Buddhadasa Bhikkhu started to develop and propagate his message of a reformed Buddhism,[1] while modern Thai literary writing in the form of the novel was slowly coming of age.

The following periods of military rule and dictatorship were not particularly favourable to the growth of social thought, but its development was irrepressible, as demonstrated by the novels of Siburapha and Seni Saowaphong, or the concern with poverty and deprivation in the Northeast that landed many of the protesters involved in jail. Slowly, new forms of social and political consciousness kept unfolding, although not necessarily overtly, and often in despite of the express wishes of those in power.

Under Marshal Sarit (1957–63), national development became the top priority (Thak, 1979); this was also the period of increasing American involvement in Vietnam, and thus in Thailand, and the beginning of the communist armed struggle in the country, a conflict in which the brilliant intellectual Jit Phumisak would become one of the first victims. The American presence, especially the excesses of troops during their often wild periods of 'Rest and Recreation', became very visible under Sarit's successors, at the same time that a modern economy was beginning to evolve. In the name of development as a means of fighting communism, vast parts of the countryside were opened up, not only to material but also to ideological modernization, whether official or clandestine. Although the intellectual climate remained repressive, the government in Bangkok had to allow for a modicum of democratic representation, but it suppressed this again in 1971.

Twenty-five years of rule by military marshals came to an end in October 1973, when protracted student demonstrations for a constitution finally escalated to the level of a confrontation with the army and police. The ensuing violence shocked the nation, but ushered in a period of unprecedented freedom during which progressive ideas of all sorts could circulate. Arts, literature, and publishing flourished, while an interestingly diverse press emerged, though at the same time the unbridled contentions between opposing political forces resulted in chaos and violence, with the division between the contestants opening up along the lines of progressive versus conservative. It was also a period of anti-American protest, and a fierce nationalism, in which all and sundry claimed to embody the principles and to be striving for the protection of the national symbols of Nation, Religion, and King.

Understanding the intellectual ferment that became visible in the 'democratic period' of 1973–76 is essential if one is to grasp the nature of the forces involved in the further economical, social, and cultural modernization of Thailand. The students 'discovered' the writings of Siburapha and Seni Saowaphong, and began to read the works of the other progressives of the 1950s, plus the socio-historical analyses of Jit Phumisak (Reynolds, 1987). In doing so, they became aware of poverty and peasants, labour and exploitation, privilege and corruption, and the necessity of critical social analysis. While doing so, these children of the elite and middle classes, on whom the army had trained its guns during the October days, realized that their world of ideas was far divorced from that of their parents' generation, and the dominant ideology in which they had been educated.

The given order of society could no longer simply be taken for granted; politics and questions of state began to become common concerns; Buddhadasa Bhikkhu-inspired Buddhist reform gained in popularity; and the genesis of new Buddhist movements, such as the Santi Asoke moral reform sect and the Thammakai meditation cum self-discipline movement, can roughly be dated to this period of intellectual agitation. It was also a time in which new lifestyles were questioned. With the presence of so many American soldiers, especially those on 'R & R', the public became aware of all sorts of entertainment activities that were neither particularly polite nor 'Thai', at the same time that the nation's political subservience to American interests was also creating widespread aversion and distrust. This confluence of blatant consumerism and alien lifestyles, allied to political dependence, resulted in the emergence of a powerful nationalistic reaction that made the country, its interests and culture, the centre of attention.

In the ensuing debates about nationalism, about what is Thai and what is un-Thai, about what to accept and what to reject, about what is desirable and what should be got rid of, the racial question sometimes also reared its head. If Americans were to blame for cultural degeneration, why not blame the Chinese for exploitation, economic ills, and their lack of nationalism and identification with the country that had brought them fortune? As attention was brought to bear on this issue, the realization dawned that it was no longer a real problem. What some Southeast Asian countries still have not yet succeeded in accomplishing had already happened in Thailand, almost without anybody noticing it: the Chinese, who still in the 1950s were highly visible as a separate ethnic group, were in the process of disappearing as such, and had begun to identify themselves as Thais.

Remarkably revealing on this is Botan's novel *Letters from Thailand* (1969), which tells the story of a Chinese immigrant who grudgingly witnesses how his children become Sino-Thais. By way of intermarriage and cultural compatibility, the integration has steadily proceeded, producing a business establishment and a middle class that is a proud mixture of the two cultures, and that by and large thinks of itself as Thai. Notable among this group have been many 'reformers', who apparently have wanted to improve upon Thai culture even though they are only one or two generations removed from their Chinese origins. They have included such critics of Thai Buddhist practice as, Buddhadasa Bhikkhu and the venerable Phothirak of the Santi Asoke sect, and social pundits, such as Puey Ungphakorn (1975), Boonsanong Punyodyana (1973), and Sulak Sivaraksa (1980), all of whom made impressive contributions to the discussions of the 1970s through their vigorous writing and publishing activities.

It is no longer purely Chinese business acumen that explains Thailand's striking and steady economic progress over the last thirty years. Apart from the important role of the government in the economy and its liberal-conservative monetary policy, business and banking have become respectable in Thai culture. In recent years the Thai and Sino-Thai business establishment has also grown to be a weighty political factor. This rapid growth, and the resultant political clout it brings, has also been accomplished by a further reciprocal interpenetration of the interests of the state, the bureaucracy, the army, and big business.

The students of the early 1970s discovered and discussed many ideas that go against the grain of Thai culture, one being 'equality' in the sense of democracy and accountable government, another being the right to education, and some have even questioned the morality of hierarchy by debating the sensitive issue of the authority of the highest in the realm, and by demonstratively refusing to participate in the Homage to Teachers ceremony. Since the moral content of hierarchical relationships is firmly grounded in the family, they were bound to fail in propagating their anti-hierarchical thinking, but what they did bring about was a more informed debate on the content of democracy and accountability, and about the right to education.

In the 1970s, the idea of open universities, accessible to everybody, was finally implemented. It has led to an education explosion that is very rapidly creating a broad, relatively educated public that nowadays makes its demands on the system felt in terms of job and employment opportunities, the calls for the realization of social justice, plus political protests, and a growing ecological movement. These newly educated people cannot in any way be absorbed by the bureaucratic system, as their forerunners were in times when higher education was a privilege of the few. Then, the expanding bureaucracy could absorb the vast majority of the graduates, and a career in government was a common prospect. All that changed at the same time that extra-governmental employment became available in a growing economy that has been shifting over from agriculture and government to tourism, communications, and industry.

It may be revealing to illustrate the magnitude of the demand for education. In 1961, it was estimated that there were 15,000 Thai university students, not counting some 2,000 studying abroad. Now, in the early nineties, it is thought that some 600,000 people are enrolled at the tertiary level, plus more than 8,000 overseas. In the process, an urban civilization is developing that is no longer in touch with its rural hinterland, or with the feudal ways of yester-year. That culture is expressed in a lively, informative and critical press, in an impressive amount of book publishing, and, of course, in a booming entertainment and fast food industry, in traffic jams, department stores, high-rises, and other demonstrations of consumer culture and economic expansion, such as fashion and design, art galleries and spectacular architecture.

Sometimes it is thought that economic expansion is a precondition for the evolution of a democratic society, but such an expansion may equally well serve conspicuous consumption, mass cultural entertainment, and a self-centred materialism that distracts attention away from democratic and critical social thinking. Compared to the 1970s, the level of political awareness in Thai society does not seem to have grown. There has been, of course, the stunning electoral success of former Bangkok overnor Chamlong Simuang's party, the Force of Righteousness, that is closely associated with the Santi Asoke sect, but it is difficult to see what else that political triumph meant beyond a general (urban) distaste for traditional politics, and the craving for a clean, efficient government.

In agreement with the dominant moralistic view of social life, the party's ideology seems to originate from the idea that the good order of society follows from individual moral awareness and conduct. In this sense it is fully in line with the other moral development programmes that prosper in the urban environment, as demonstrated by the burgeoning of the various Buddhist reform movements and the ongoing, official campaign that promotes the wholesome—western, middle-class—family as the ideal basic construction block of a desirable society. Yet, it remains hard to imagine what implications, if any, such raising of moral awareness might have in terms of societal reorganization.

Technocracy and the expanding economy seem to have led to political indifference, at least among the general public, and to extra-governmental protests and activities, for instance, of environmentalists, or social welfare activities of Non-Governmental Organizations (NGOs), which have multiplied dramatically in recent years. The agendas of such groups seem to be confined to dealing with symptoms rather than examining the system that produces them, and they normally fall short in ideological or theoretical sophistication. That is, they do not seem to have developed a sociological picture of society, where things are interconnected, but instead loosely blame 'capitalist development' for all social ills.

The high level of political awareness of the 1970s was expressed in student radicalism, by the students' efforts to connect with life in the countryside and to politically awaken the rural population, by a massive production of 'social realist' literature, and the composition of hundreds of 'songs for life', such as those performed by the travelling student group Caravan. This has changed. At present, most students seem to prepare themselves for a career in society rather than for changing it, and if they are politically active, they tend to protest corruption or the abuse of 'democracy'; if they are active at the grass roots' level, they are typically engaged in NGO activities which, more often than not, try to learn from the experience of life in the countryside rather than to impose urban political views on the villagers.

In parallel with Thailand's economic development, an urban working class culture seems to be in the making. While a huge proportion of the urban work force still consists of migratory labour that maintains a close relationship with the countryside and its culture, for a gradually expanding number of people the city has become home, and factory or harbour the 'natural' places of work. Unionism, labour action, and a good measure of class consciousness have become part of their prospect. Instead of the elitist

11

Caravan of the 1970s, it is the more earthy Carabao Thai-rock group that expresses their thoughts and aspirations.

Other urban subcultures that are springing up as by-products of a booming modern sector, and the money that it generates, are the condominium yuppie lifestyle, and an emerging youth culture. Such subcultures only partly generate their own idiom, and give rise to a culture industry that produces the items, symbols, and entertainment that a certain public is said to need. In the urban environment, this may range from luxury apartments and flashy cars to modern forms of fast food, audience specific types of music with their song books, movies, star cults, and scores of magazines that tell people how to live and what to want. The amount of social criticism contained in these approximates to zero.

So, during the period under consideration, we have witnessed enormous changes in Thai life. From a dual structure of society, the estate of the noble rulers and that of the peasantry, Thai society has gradually developed a considerable degree of diversification and social differentiation. This is especially apparent in the modern urban environment. Its culture sets the pace for the rest of the country, sending the population at large messages about how life can and should be lived, of what things to aspire to.

The cultural influence of modern Bangkok is sustained by the administrative reforms of the late nineteenth century and the ensuing, and still ongoing, rather uniform penetration of society by the state. As this went on, the previously autonomous peripheral regions were integrated with the centre, and by now regional cultural variation is declining at an accelerating pace. Recently, it was discovered that local differences may stimulate tourism so, since a few years back, every province boasts a cultural office to promote the 'characteristic' features of the area. This, of course, does not detract from the fact that, leaving aside hill tribes and southern Moslems, a very recognizable, nation-wide modern Thai culture is developing, meshed together by an increasingly extensive system of communications, whether by road or rail, by broadcast media or the press, a centralized system of school education, and by the effective diffusion of nationalism and its symbols.

While this national integration may be described as an internal opening up of the country as a by-product of centralized administration, the development of communications, and an expanding economy,[2] the country is also unfolding more and more to influences from abroad, not only by responding to impulses from the world economy, but also by taking in quantities of new ideas, new technology, new ways of doing things, and new consumption patterns. It also absorbs, temporarily, some six million foreign tourists a year and, less temporarily, a very large number of expatriate workers, mostly employed in the cosmopolitan Bangkok metropolis. Simultaneously, more and more Thais have been gaining first hand experience of foreign countries, not only through tourism and study on the part of the more well-to-do, but also through massive labour migration to Singapore, Japan, the Middle East, Europe, and the United States. Thais have now spread out pretty well everywhere, and they bring their experiences back home with them when they return.

This opening up to the world has been a most spectacular movement, especially over the last thirty years. As recently as the fifties, it was almost impossible to find English speakers outside two or three elite university campuses; tourists were uncommon; social scientific knowledge about the country was in its infancy; Thai-speaking foreigners were rarities; the press was subdued and inward looking. Which is to say that, while not exactly complacent, Thai society still gave an impression of cultural self-sufficiency, providing its own idiom and content for its national discourse, while only occasionally being disturbed by new ideas voiced by the few who had studied abroad for years. Naturally, the rather repressive regimes of the military marshals did their best to keep things just the way they were.

Probably the most powerful single factor that led to the opening up of society was America's massive involvement in Vietnam, soon followed by the consequences of economic growth and the education explosion. In the 1970s, international tourism reached Southeast Asia in a big way, and labour migration began in earnest. All this affected the world of ideas, first among students, but then for many others, too. The resulting discourse was one in which a developing quality press played and continues to play a highly significant role. But while all this was going on, the rapid and continuous growth of consumer culture, with its fetish called lifestyles, was also observable.

Now the question that has arisen is whether this opening up, internally and to the external world, is threatening to deform Thai culture and its style, whether these will be 'modernized' in the process of the globalization of culture to the point of becoming a mere caricature of their time-hallowed image. Although there are Thai social critics who warn that Thai society is on its way to losing its own identity, while prescribing, for instance, the serious practice of Buddhism as an antidote to alien influences, most Thais are rather confident, as they always have been, that future developments will be adapted to the Thai way of life rather than that this way will suffer from its contact with foreign elements.

This cultural self-confidence is perhaps typically Thai, along with a good measure of skill in pragmatic adaptation. They still like a well-regulated style of life, just as before, which not only involves a bent for aestheticism, but also the appreciation of harmonious social order, in which is implicit respect for interpersonal relationships and hierarchy, and the ensuing rights and obligations; all this is also expressed in pleasant manners, and the proverbial smile. Of course, many people in Bangkok have stopped smiling, but generally they are polite and expect other people to be polite in return, and the expectation that society should be orderly remains.

Sometimes the Thai predilection for order and a decorous style of life is violated by their encounters with western tourists. For instance, until the new airport terminal was finished, the first thing tourists saw, while waiting to get their passports stamped, was a sign displaying a long list of presentational requirements, specifying how foreigners should dress and look if they did not want to be treated as 'hippies'—the implication being that the latter would find themselves at the end of every queue: no to shorts and singlets, no to open sandals and long hair, and so forth. It did not deter the tourists from coming to the immigration officials in attire that seemed more suited for a holiday at the beach than for a visit to the national capital. Naturally, they are not allowed to enter the royal palace that way, but I have never seen anybody ordered out of a government office for not respecting the Thai dress code. So in the Thai way, if one cannot win by admonition, one should either get tough or find a compromise. It is, perhaps, noteworthy that these regulations are no longer posted up in the new arrival hall.

Tourism, and thus being exposed to the view and judgment of alien others, has on occasion highlighted both Thai concerns about order and decorum and also their sense of pragmatism. The opening of a new road from Chiang Mai to Chiang Rai incidentally brought the shrine of a powerful female spirit to the attention of all passers-by, including foreigners. This irritated the local District Officer, because the offering that this particular spirit prefers in return for her granting favours is a replica of a penis, and those phalluses soon accumulate in remarkable piles in front of such shrines. The D.O. had a sign put up; "Please offer flowers only". Of course, no local devotee would be so foolish as to risk the spirit's wrath by making unwanted offerings like this. Later, when the Bangkok Hilton Hotel, honouring the terms of agreement reached when purchasing the land, kept a similar shrine in its compound, and even made it a tourist attraction, the northern District Officer's sign was taken down.

New possibilities for expressing Thai aestheticism are made available by the tourist trade too, such as in the production of beautiful and well-crafted souvenirs with very inventive designs. They are also offered by the increasing prosperity of many in the countryside, who invest in renewing rustic local temples or in constructing new ones. The building boom in glittering religious structures is highly visible as these showy edifices embody the villagers' pride and satisfy their taste for vivid and elaborate decorations. It also makes clear that in rural Thailand religion is alive and well, that people continue to invest in merit, and that the traditional way of seeking some education for the rural poor by (temporarily) entering the monkhood, is still valid: the ratio of monks and novices to population has changed only very slightly over the past twenty-five years.[3]

Religious interest remains inspired by the same old spirit and is directed to blessing and protection. The trade in amulets is as lively as ever, and the guardian spirit shrines erected in front of the new business buildings in Bangkok seem to vie against each other in size and ostentation. And it is not only in the areas of religion and aestheticism that the Thais remain very Thai indeed. There is a growing interest in their own history, not just for the sake of the nostalgia that is expressed in the many 'coffee-table books', but also at the deeper and more serious level of an interest in the elements that go to make up their own identity, which some feel is under challenge in the modern world—the recently established National Identity Board in the Prime Minister's Office being a good example.

Materialism has made rapid inroads in Thailand, of late at an almost explosive rate. Inevitably, such a change has brought new problems in its train. The rape of nature has led to erosion and serious hydrological problems. Bangkok's traffic appears close to gridlock jams, and one wonders what further urbanization is going to bring. There seems to be no end in sight to the building boom with office and apartment blocks rising higher and higher all the time. While the need for decentralization is a common topic these days, it remains to be seen whether the powers-that-be will ever consent to this innovation, since it runs counter to their own interests—all the reins of power can run through their hands only for as long as Bangkok reigns supreme. The determined centralization of authority is a policy that has been followed by every government since 1892, one side-effect of which has been the conversion of a green tropical city into a concrete jungle that can only function by the use of air-conditioning. In short, there is no lack of manifestations of 'modernity' and unrestricted economic development, all of which are affecting the quality of life.

In spite of all this, the Thais also remain impressively their own. Whatever the changes and problems, they seem to cope in a self-assured way that may strike outsiders as surprisingly nonchalant in relation to the scale of societal problems. Perhaps this is related to the dichotomization of life's experience into an area that really matters and that concerns one's immediate personal relationships, and public life that is thought to be a matter of state and government, far away entities that are beyond the reach and control of individual citizens. Consequently, public control is still weakly developed, a fact that increasingly gives big business the opportunities to manipulate the political process, in transactions largely obscured from public view.

The consumer culture is not exactly helpful to any who might be eager to foster the growth of the checks and balances of public control and civic-mindedness. Politics is something to watch, a spectator sport that may be exciting, but it still has to go a long way if it is to evolve to the stage where party programmes, platform politics, and the representation of the public interest in its all diversity are included in its dimensions. Politically, the main contemporary goal seems to be more and more economic expansion, with the resulting goodies to be shared out among those who are part of the 'modern sector'. But the pursuit of this objective has also created a vast gap between urban affluence and rural poverty that is reminiscent of the old, two-estates structure of society, in which some had all the privilege and control over resources, while the others were allowed to suffer and to serve. Meanwhile, though, society has grown in complexity and in possibilities for individual advancement. It is these opportunities for social mobility and material progress rather than political reform that preoccupy the minds of most.

The development of political culture

The ascent to power of the tycoon Chatchai Chunhawan in Thailand in 1988 was also hailed by many as a victory for democracy, because Chatchai was a popularly elected prime minister and his cabinet consisted in the main of civilian businessmen. What's more, the Thai economy was booming and continued to grow rapidly thereafter. But are there any good reasons to suppose that there is a causal connection between business, economic development, and democracy?

The belief that there is such a connection may be inspired by reflections on the western experience, and most especially on the role of the bourgeoisie in its emancipation from dynastic control and the subsequent growth of a civil society, in which democratic processes came to control government and state. We should, perhaps, question if this model does not sound simply too good to be true. It may also be asked whether a 'civil society' ever existed in which a real participatory democracy prevailed. Seen from a class viewpoint, this can never have been in the interests of a capitalist bourgeoisie.

There is no necessary connection identifiable between business, its growth, and democracy. What counts in the political process everywhere, and very clearly so in Southeast Asia, is belonging to the in-group of political decision-makers. And what goes on inside the back-rooms of the halls of power remains rather murky and obscure to the public. It is not a public affair in spite of the trappings of democracy. No, business is not going to make the world a more democratic place, even now when it has obviously penetrated the Southeast Asian bastions of politics. Businessmen are now among the 'ins', but not all who are in business are in, nor is it always the same people who are influential, as the experience of Chatchai's political and business associates illustrates.[4]

In Thailand, we find an emergent educated public—probably the most essential ingredient for a democratic society—that tries to produce a politically effective public opinion. Because its members write in and to the newspapers, and are active on the NGO scene, their voices can often be heard. Their political influence is weak, however. Meanwhile, though, with education becoming available on an impressive scale, popular opinion will come to be a more important factor, but it is still debatable whether it will result in a politically enlightened public. For this is also a time when the economy, and 'development at all cost', dominate the thinking of politicians and government alike, while issues of staying afloat, mobility, and raising one's standard of living preoccupy most individuals. For the majority, it is the stark matter of survival that counts, but for a considerable minority, their anxieties concern status considerations, leading to increased consumption.

Consumer culture in a semi-anonymous environment does not make for responsible citizenship or the growth of democracy. The education invested serves individuals' accumulative skills, rather than fostering the desire to participate in national affairs. Thus, as long as the government legitimizes itself by stimulating economic expansion and the opportunity for personal advancement of the educated segment of the public, its members will be more interested in their private affairs than in creating politically relevant public opinion and debate.

So, while it would be going too far to say that public opinion is entirely irrelevant in Thai politics, in order to grasp the nature of the political process there, the observer should not let himself be deceived by the democratic window-dressing. The relevant questions to ask about political development are: Who is in power? Who are the 'ins'? Which are the groups, institutions, or establishments that can effectively manipulate the political process and the state? But the observer should also bear in mind that the 'ins' are changing; new interests get 'in', older interests may decline in importance, sometimes unexpected moralists get in and gain access to the levers of power, perhaps even in the name of democracy or democratization.

The 'ins'

When Thai royal absolutism was replaced by constitutional government in 1932, those who led the revolt to achieve emancipation from royal prerogatives were mostly the foreign-educated elements in the military and bureaucracy. The centralized bureaucratic polity that had been organized toward the end of the nineteenth century was firmly in place, and continued to expand and dominate society in conjunction with the military establishment (Riggs, 1966). The tendency toward centralization of state control continued unabated and, in cooperation with the largely Chinese commercial class, the state claimed a prominent role in the economy.

Since then, other groups have come to the fore who demand a say in the polity. During the unruly and nationalistic open society of 1973–76, demands for social justice, popular participation in the political process, and accountability of government were forcefully expressed. Naturally, the initiative was with university students, supported by broad popular movements. At the same time, and on up into the present, the business community has been pressing for a share in power and, for the first time, openly dominated the political process from 1988 to February 1991.

A more recent element in Thai politics is the emergence of a political party that bases itself on moral issues and popular consensus. This party is the Phalang Tham (Force of Righteousness) that originally brought Brigadier-General Chamlong Simuang to the governorship of the Thai metropolis. Nicknamed 'Mr Clean' or 'Holy Monk', due to his prominence in the unorthodox Buddhist (moral revival) movement Santi Asoke, the population overwhelmingly voted him into power, much to the displeasure of the traditional political establishment, who subsequently tried to obstruct Chamlong's policies, and even moved against the Santi Asoke independent monkhood. None of this discouraged the electorate from renewing Chamlong's mandate in 1989 with a landslide victory, not only because of his moral stature, but also due to his energetic tackling of urban problems. Since that time, the Phalang Tham has developed from a regional, Bangkok-based party into a national one and has been part and parcel of the civilian coalition governments from 1992 to 1997.[5]

Before that time, however, the military reared its ugly head once again. Protesting the excesses of the 'business-ism' and 'crony-ism' of the Chatchai government; irritated at the appointment of controversial advisors to the prime minister's office; and with the army being ignored as a social force, General Suchinda Khraprayun and his classmates staged a coup and installed the National Peace-Keeping Council (NPKC). As usual in the history of the many military take-overs in Thailand, it was justified by the promise of restoring order and the drafting of a new, more adequate constitution. Of course, the men in green said not to desire power for its own sake. Be that as it may, the move was initially well received by the population and disenfranchised competitors, and also, importantly, not opposed by the King.

The true colours of the NPKC became clear, at first by its severely curtailing the rights and democratic space of labour, then in the drawn-out constitution drafting process in which the military claimed an important, permanent role in parliament. When finally, against all his repeated assertions to the contrary, General Suchinda arrogated the prime-ministership to himself, popular indignation, fired by the provocative hunger strike of the Palang Tham leader Chamlong, came to a head. It resulted in massive middle-class demonstrations that were fired upon by Suchinda's henchmen—killing fifty to two hundred unarmed civilians. Shortly after this massacre, the general-turned-prime minister amnestied himself, and stepped down.

The indiscriminate killings and the freedom from prosecution of the perpetrators have caused a national trauma and soul-searching that have not come to their end. The fact that the army is discredited, however, does not mean that it can be ignored, although the heyday of the political military is now behind us. Of all political forces, the business establishment, with its godfather-leaders (*chaopho*; Chai-anan, 1991:78–80), remains in the ascendency, with the 1995–96 prime minister, Banhan Sinlapa-acha, as its epitome. Also the instruments of the state remain important political players, and among these it is not just the bureaucracy. Many members of the former NPKC still exert considerable influence, which is best illustrated by the recent co-optation of General Suchinda on the board of one of the most powerful conglomerates. The state, represented by the bureaucracy and the military, and the economy, appearing as business in its widest sense, need each other and share many common interests (Chai-anan and Suchit, 1985). Along with these, the monarch at the apex performs an important function too, one that is simultaneously political and moral. In its moral-charismatic aspect—the ruler symbolizing the nation—the king's role is to bridge the gap between the power elite at the centre and the populace at large.

The political centre stage, however, is hidden from public view, and its actors do not feel accountable to a population, whom they expect to be apolitical. Yet, sometimes, groups do muster around issues of gross exploitation, and may demonstrate or strike for better wages and conditions of work, or against foreclosure and military-backed dam-building and reforestation. Other, moral, forms of political organization typically organize vertically, cutting across class lines—Chamlong's Force of Right-eousness being a perfect example. Engaged in by members of the educated urban middle classes, this type of activism protests corruption, arbitrariness, military arrogance, the power of business, the destruction of the environment, the absence of social justice, or human rights abuses. For the time being, to what extent these various forms of mobilization and protest against established political practice will be effective in penetrating, or influencing, the political centre stage remains to be seen.

Towards a civil culture of the public world?

Among members of the urban middle classes different ideas about the order of wider society have taken root, and these people may share an interest in instituting the rule of law, administrative predictability, political accountability, and government inspired by a vision of the common welfare. In other words, among members of these classes a civil society, and the idea of a common *res publica*, is developing.

The public issues concerned are typically discussed by academicians, students, and professionals who are in contact with the global world of ideas, but often this intelligentsia has difficulty in relating their ideas to the specific situation of Thai society. Despite this, their arguments may prove persuasive to other members of those broad and largely powerless middle classes, like the modern professionals, clerics, civil servants, and *petite bourgeoisie*, alongside sometimes even higher levels, such as disenfranchised big business, and other opponents of the regime.

The debates are typically conducted in the press, but are still weak in sociological analysis: this involves consciousness of structure, of history, of institutions, and the concept of legitimacy in order to be able to identify the root causes of the political economy's problems and obstacles confronting it. So far, such theoretical and ideological consciousness is only at the nascent stage. All concerns are still gut issues, and the typical moralistic commentary of the newspaper pundits is simplistic rather than practicable. The fact that 'public' topics are now being aired, though, and some thinking about solutions is taking place, is new in itself. The recognition of problems, and the expression of people's concerns about them, are the first steps in the creation of a relevant public opinion. Discussing difficulties raises consciousness and, in the process, society at large is elevated from the domain of the taken-for-granted everyday life into a realm of challenge and responsibility, one that concerned citizens desire to bring under their own control.

Historically, the most important contribution toward the development of the public debate on society and its problems, on social justice and the common weal, has been made by progressive intellectuals and socialist parties. This political left is marginal and unobtrusive in Thailand, not because of censorship or suppression, but since it seems to have run its turbulent course between the mid-sixties and the early eighties. At present, it is hardly stirring as a political organization, and Phalang Tham-style moralism, plus the expediencies of state and economy, may be enough to keep progressive intellectuals or labour removed from the centre of politics.

It would be a mistake to expect the initial stages in the evolution of a civil culture of the public world to be evident in the explicitly political realm. Civic action already exists alongside the political and administrative sphere of the state, and is typically organized in all sorts of NGOs, in ecological activism, feminism, anti-corruption campaigns, and other such cause-orientations or issues. As such, they breathe a civic spirit, yet, since they are typically issues-oriented, they do not address the problems of society within an encompassing ideological frame, and those involved generally concentrate on symptoms rather than causes.

Taken all together, one thus sees the flowering of a counter-culture protesting the political status quo. The overriding concerns seem to be the imparting of a moral, consensual element to the exercise of power; the fight against poverty and its causes; the establishment of credible democratic processes; the promotion of social justice; and the rule of law; in sum, the creation of a civil culture of the public world with the involvement of a responsible participatory citizenship.

As of now, participatory citizenship that is able to influence the political centre does not yet exist, and it will encounter formidable obstacles in its realization, such as the power of inertia inherent in the present organization of the political economy, and well-entrenched political interest groups that will not easily be dislodged. What has come about so far is the growth of alternative thinking about politics, an emerging vision of how the future should be. This new social reality seems firmly ensconced.

The main trend, however, seems to be toward a media-dominated consumer society, at least for those who have entered the modern sector. The life of the others can only be described as an endless, yet persistent, struggle for survival. With economic concerns overriding in the minds of most, the demand for participatory politics seems likely to remain subdued, while the civil culture of the public world will concern itself more with moral protest and cause-oriented civic action than with effective political reform.

CHAPTER 2

POWER AND GOODNESS IN THAI SYMBOLIC REPRESENTATIONS

Analysis

In Thai thinking, Buddhism deals essentially with virtue and wisdom, which can liberate people from the common order of life. Buddhism shows the way out of the fetters of existence which, for our purposes, means the human condition that is characterized by impermanence, suffering, and an illusory self that is subject to the cycle of rebirth (*samsara*). It transcends and relates to the trustworthy order of morality and goodness that is symbolized by the home, the mother, and the female symbols of Mother Earth and Mother Rice. Both the Buddha and also these latter three female entities are considered to have the highest *phrakhun* (goodness) towards us, its beneficiaries; together they constitute the domain of moral goodness, or what I call the '*khuna* dimension of existence'.

	Khuna ('moral goodness')			*Decha* ('power')	
Order	Pure order	Order of goodness		Tenuous order	Chaos
Symbol	The Buddha	The mother	interpenetration	*Saksit* power	Evil
Quality	Pure virtue; stillness	Deeply moral		Amoral	Immoral
		Safety		Protential danger.	

Domesticated area of existence

24

Next to this domain, we find the realm of supernatural power and, first, the area that the Thais classify as *saksit*. This realm is much less trustworthy and does not necessarily have moral characteristics; it represents the tenuous order outside the home. It is the subject of the most intensive religious preoccupation—concerning loss and gain, danger and protection—and there are very clear, almost mechanical, rules for dealing with it. Beyond the area of *saksit* power, we find the area of chaos and extreme unreliability, represented by the fearsome spectre of pure wickedness and immorality. Together, these latter two kinds of power form the '*decha* dimension of existence', while in between the *khuna* and *decha* dimensions, we find an area of intermingling that affects the safety and continuity of the group. Schematically all this can be ordered as follows:

Decha

Domesticated power

Power is the most spectacular, beguiling, and central manifestation of Thai life; its cognitive elaborations and the way power is accommodated reveal the essentially animistic substratum of the Thai mentality. An understanding of *saksit* power will provide us with an ordering principle against which other classifications can be understood.

Power is primarily vested in *sing saksit* (sacred objects), such as Buddha images, stupas *(chedi)*, temple buildings, amulets, mantras, holy water, the spirits and the gods *(phisang thewada)*, and in the shrines in which they are immanent. Sometimes power is also vested in out-of-the-ordinary manifestations of nature, such as white elephants or deformed babies. *Saksit* power is also inherent in the position of the king, and as a matter of principle, in everything that has mysterious qualities. This power is both potentially beneficent and harmful; it lies all around us, like the atmosphere, and when it condenses in places or objects it results in *singsaksit*. People have to come to an accommodation with this sphere of power and must approach it on its own terms, in accordance with the laws that guide it. The power of *sing saksit* can be tapped for personal purposes, its protection may be sought, and its vengeful manifestations can be neutralized.

In almost every house compound, there is the small and attractive spirit shrine of the *phraphum*. *Phraphum* is 'the lord of the place' *(chaothi)*, that is, the local ruler whose presence should be recognized and respected. Just as all goods have their owner, all places have their local lord, not because of a higher order of legitimation, but as a matter of fact and natural right. The incidental human occupants of a compound therefore need to pay respect to the local potentate in order to be safe and to avoid its wrath, which can be provoked by negligent or disrespectful behaviour. If respected, well treated, and occasionally feasted, the *phraphum* will be protective in return and care for the safety of the place. If untoward incidents still happen, these cannot be the fault of the spirit, and in such cases the causes need to be sought elsewhere.

Phraphum is not the only local lord: in a village one will find at least two others, the *phiban*, that is, the ruler and protector of the village territory and also the *phiwat*, or *suawat*, that is, the guardian spirit of the temple compound. These lords should also be respected and honoured, and their beneficial protection needs to be sought periodically. Similarly, the wider territory of the province has its *saksit* ruler and protector, the *phimuang* or *sua-muang* that resides in or at the city pillar or *lakmuang*.

While the above might suggest that there is a hierarchy among the local lords, there does not appear to be any strict order of precedence among these potentates; they are simply there, exercising their right to rule. They all want to be respected and they all need to be supplicated in order to ensure the welfare of the human beings in their territory. The little *phraphum* of one's house compound, being nearest, may easily be the most important of all since he is directly in charge of the protection of those who live in his immediate surroundings. A *phraphum* is certainly not satisfied with respect paid to the *sua-muang* or the *phiban* but wants to be respected in his own right. Because of his proximity, his subjects had best respect his wishes.

These guardian spirits are basically local rulers who have no power outside of their respective territories; in other places one needs to deal with other local potentates. But their power, too, is very much confined to their respective shrines, or ritual centres. One needs to go to these to supplicate them or tap their power since with increasing distance, it dissipates accordingly and they have no influence outside the borders of their realm. Some university students may seek success in examinations at the shrine of the *phraphum* of the university compound, but there is little use in seeking the blessing of guardian spirits when one is outside their sphere of influence. In other words, it is not very practical or politic for a traveller to remain devoted to the guardian spirit of his village when he is away. As soon as he steps outside his village boundaries, he enters the realm of another local ruler who must be respected and worshipped.

While guardian spirits that care for the general peacefulness and protection of their territory are localized by definition, there are other entities which, for instance, see to the growth of rice and the falling of rain; these *thewada* influence and regulate specific processes. But however widespread their activities may be, these forces should be addressed at the right time and place if their blessing is to be invoked. There is little point in seeking the protection or curative properties of the miraculous relic of the Buddha at Doi Suthep Temple in Chiang Mai without going there, and one does not ensure good luck by praying to the Four-Faced Brahma *(Thao Maha Phrom)* housed at the Erawan Hotel in Bangkok while one is up-country. The supplicant had better go to its shrine to propitiate a powerful spirit if he wants to feel any assurance. All these powers, be they guardian spirits, powerful Buddha images, or rulers of certain realms of activity, are basically localized and their protection should be sought at their particular shrines.[1]

In order to invoke the benevolent attention of *saksit* forces, the worshipper must initiate the transaction by paying respect and making a small offering. The supplicant then offers his terms of contract: if the concerned entity will fulfil his wishes, he will return and offer a feast, a pig's head, flowers, or perhaps even a theatrical performance. Most *saksit* powers have known likes and dislikes: the Buddha image *Phra Phuttha-chinnarat* in Phitsanulok likes pigs' heads, *Phra Kaeo Morakot* (The Emerald Buddha) loves hard boiled eggs, the spirit of the city pillar in Bangkok is fond of *la-khon chatri* performances, and the Four-Faced Brahma at the Erawan Hotel appreciates flower garlands, elephant statues, and a donation to the Erawan Hospital Foundation. Female spirits *(chaomae)* have a marked predilection for phalli.

The ritual of the invocation is always the same: one first pays respect and makes a small offering of burning incense in order to attract attention, then one states one's wish and makes a vow, and finally, after being granted one's wishes, redeems the vow. According to Phraya Anuman Rajadon, "If a *thewada* does not want to give what it has been asked for, but the ceremonial way in which it has been supplicated was correct, then it must without reservation fulfil that wish".[2] The contract between a supplicant and a protective spirit or *thewada*, or any other thing classified as *singsaksit*, is largely mechanical, for a specific purpose, and of relatively short duration.

The *saksit* forces respond to presentation, such as right ceremony, proper words, appropriate movements and formulae, and people generally know how to perform their side of the contract. Its efficacy is not inherent in itself but rather in their knowledge of the correct form that makes *thewada* and benevolent spirits respond. These entities may therefore be considered to be domesticated: people have clear ideas on how to handle them and are familiar with their behaviour; in this sense they are reliable and predictable. The same predictability is expected of the human participant in the contract. When a favour has been sought against a promise, the *saksit* entity concerned may become very irritated and dangerous if the vow is not redeemed in the correct manner and according to the terms of contract. In such cases, it turns vengeful and will punish negligent behaviour.

Insult to *saksit* forces is by no means sinful, but merely stupid. One does not activate karmic retribution by defaulting on a businesslike contract but, in the manner of a civil lawsuit, the problem will be settled between the concerned parties. To honour the terms of contract is beneficial, while the folly of not doing so will result in revenge, disaster, shame and loss of face. *Saksit* forces are highly sensitive about their power, rank, and prestige; they are easily insulted, yet also easy to please by a show of respect, an offer, or a bribe.

Summarizing, we find that the concept of *saksit* has the following attributes. The human life situation is encompassed by a realm of nature and supernature in which power is vested. Humans need it for protection, for blessing, for safety and auspiciousness, and for success in their personal and communal pursuits. In places such as shrines or other sacred localities, and in objects such as amulets, power is concentrated. This condensation becomes addressable and manifests itself as *singsaksit*. By knowing the proper method, such as the use of rituals, ceremonies, or incantations, these potencies can be induced to work for the needs of the human supplicants. Consequently, they may be considered to be domesticated. Contracts with such entities are defined by their purpose, have a relatively short time perspective, and need to be periodically renewed. *Saksit* forces are potentially benevolent and protective, but can be dangerous, jealous and vengeful if they feel slighted. In spite of these characteristics, humans feel the need to depend on them and seek their favour. To do so, the human partner must be the one to initiate the transaction.

Basically, *saksit* power is amoral, because it does not concern itself with motives and serves the good and the wicked alike. It is unprincipled and reacts to mechanical manipulation and an outward show of respect. Contracts with it are guided by a businesslike logic, and there is no higher moral principle that guides these. Moreover, these agreements are never fully reliable. If insulted, *saksit* beings may turn dangerous and seek revenge, but that revenge is escapable if its victim places himself under the protection of other more powerful supernatural agents, takes refuge in the monkhood, or simply leaves their sphere of influence. Therefore, to attempt to take advantage of *saksit* forces by, for instance, failing to redeem a vow is not considered to be sinful or subject to the moral law of Karma. In such cases one merely exposes oneself to revenge, which is plain stupid.

Nondomesticated power

Next to the *saksit* forces that are somewhat ambivalent but potentially benevolent, we find the inauspicious, wicked and evil representatives of the realm of chaos and immorality. These are the 'nondomesticated' or largely uncontrollable and often 'roaming' forces that are the carriers of bad luck. These evil spirits are unpredictable and essentially malevolent. They tend to act of their own volition rather than to wait until properly and ceremonially addressed; they resemble criminals and trouble-makers. Before they can be neutralized or mastered, they will usually have done some harm, having caused illness, death, destruction, or simply terror and fright. They can only be controlled with a strong counter force, such as a Pali incantation *(khatha)* by a Buddhist monk, or through the mediations of a spirit doctor. The latter specializes in localizing the spirit, and then subduing it by trapping it in a pot, or chasing it away by evoking strong annulling forces. These fiends can sometimes also be dealt with by politely placating them and asking them to go away in return for a gift—essentially a pay-off. But when all remedies fail, people had better lie low and try not to give further offence, in the hope that the carrier of inauspiciousness will roam on.

Some spectres are believed to be vaguely localized in places, such as cemeteries or forests, and are a nuisance or danger to the traveller beyond the protection of his guardian spirit or a *thewada*. To cope with such a threat, the traveller may surround himself with the portable *saksit* power of amulets, tattoos, and various protective formulae. Most often these amulets and words are of Buddhist inspiration, such as small Buddha amulets *(phra khruang)*, medals *(rian phra)* of famous and spiritually powerful monks, and passages from Pali texts.[3] Protective tattoos are most often of mixed Brahmanic and Buddhist origin. Whatever the form, the protective power is not located in a person but in an outside agent that he has obtained. To acquire protection, invulnerability, or prosperity, one depends at least as much on these external *saksit* agents as on one's own skill, merit or plain good luck.

The most effective means to confront evil, immorality and chaos, are the powerful 'white magic' symbols that derive from the realm of moral goodness (see *Khuna* below). Whereas protection against evil may be sought through propitiation of benevolent spirits and *thewada*, the most effective *sing saksit* derive from the symbols of moral goodness. Monks with psychic power and very charismatic laymen *(phumibun)*, by virtue of their accumulated merit, may produce powerful amulets, apply tattoos, or teach protective formulae. Similarly, relics of one's parents, and Buddha images infused with *saksit* potency, will normally protect against evil. Generally, Buddhist symbols are thought to be the most effective devices, and if a spirit doctor fails in his struggle against a representative of evil, the Buddhist monk is thought to be the ultimate agent to vanquish malevolent spirits.

In a similar sense, a village community may nurture auspiciousness and feel itself protected by the strength of merit that is generated and accumulated in the village temple. The discipline of the monks, their chanting and preaching, the merit-making ceremonies and the power vested in the Buddha image: all serve to increase the ambience of security, continuity, and auspiciousness in a life situation surrounded by potentially harmful agents. In contrast to the more transient nature of the purely animistic seats of power, the power that is vested in merit and Buddhist symbols extends over a longer time and is continuously reinforced by the presence of monks and the performance of ritual.

The power of Buddhism is most clearly demonstrated on the occasion of the supreme confrontation with chaos—death. While there are many animistic and Brahmanic elements in Thai death ritual *(phithi awa-mongkhon)*, the observances to restore order and ensure the well-being of the deceased and those left behind are clearly of Buddhist derivation.

As a religious practice, Thai animism is essentially a system that deals with power, whether of the amoral, ambivalent *saksit* or the immoral, evil variety. Such power encountered during the course of everyday life should be dealt with according to its own laws—laws which do not raise moral questions of good and evil. Whether the religious complexes that deal with such power are classified as animistic, Brahmanic, or Buddhist is irrelevant, because the way in which they deal with power is inspired by the same animistic mindset. In that mentality, supernatural forces do not question intentions but react reflexively to a show of respect, to ritual prescriptions and to ceremonial form. They can be hoodwinked by pretensions, by a nickname or a mask; they do not distinguish between the genuine and the false.

The emphasis on proper form in the contracts with powerful entities makes it very understandable that attitudes of devotion, piety, and deep emotion are generally, though not necessarily, absent while relating to them. There is no value in these attitudes because transactions are mechanical and thus superficial. The strongest emotions that a representation of power can expect to excite are reverent awe and fear *(krengklua)*. Yet to have the feeling of being protected may stimulate genuine feelings of loyalty and gratefulness on the part of the supplicant. On the other hand, equally heartfelt feelings of suffering from evil power also occur. But placating evil forces normally hinges on form and not faith, and the small, powerless man who can magically trick the powerful into favourable response may be much admired.

Power is there to supplicate and to grasp. In this way of thinking, man becomes a force in proportion to his ability to harness power. The dealings are businesslike, favour for favour, and revenge returned for insult. Power is not subject to moral restraints, because moral restraints play no part in it; it is there to be used, and the person who does not avail himself of a presented opportunity is merely foolish.

Khuna

Moral goodness

Power is complemented by moral goodness *(khun-ngam khwamdi)*. The realm of moral goodness is not antithetical to the realm of power, but the two mutually complement each other. Both are needed in life and both belong to everyday experience even though their essential characteristics are polar. Where power has a multitude of supernatural projections, goodness is most often revealed in natural and human manifestations. While power has its being in a tenuous amoral order and immoral chaos, goodness derives from moral reliability and stability. Whereas power is aggressive and largely masculine, moral goodness is powerless and its symbols are usually familiar and feminine, located squarely in this world.

The primary symbol of moral goodness is the self-sacrificing attachment of a mother to her children. She cannot help but be good, cannot but give and care; she is always benevolent and forgiving. She feeds and loves without expectation of return; she gives without asking and provides her dependents with stability and continuity in life. She is a refuge, a haven of safety, and the first to mould the moral identity of her offspring. At mother's side one is safe and knows that one will always be accepted.

In a similar vein, the earth on which we depend for our existence, the rice that feeds us, the water that sustains life, and the guardian angel that protects the young child, are all represented as female: *Mae Thorani, Mae Phosop, Mae Khongkha,* and *Mae Su.* All these life-sustaining manifestations are thought to have extraordinary goodness *(phrakhun)* towards their dependents. That benevolence engenders a moral debt that should be acknowledged; it is the fountain-head from which moral obligation arises.

In the group of representatives of moral goodness, we also find the figure of the teacher who shares the same qualities. The life-sustaining gift of the teacher is the knowledge and wisdom that his pupils need to lead a moral life. He is also thought to be a source of *metta karuna*, of sympathy and kindness, who makes considerable self-sacrifice for the good of his pupils, thus creating a moral debt on their part.

We have already seen that the *saksit* forces may have temporary moral *khun* (goodness, usefulness) to those people who place themselves under their protection, and that receiving this *khun* results in temporary obligation. The figures of moral goodness, however, obtain enduring *khun*, that is, pure *bunkhun*, vis-à-vis their charges; these wards do not need to plead but rather receive without asking. The recipients of this *bunkhun* need not fear revenge from the figures of goodness, because they will not—and cannot—avenge themselves. *Nerakhun*, that is, ingratitude or the refusal to acknowledge the moral goodness that one has received, is to sin against the dependable order of morality, and will automatically be punished by the principle of moral justice, called Karma. Psychologically, such negative behaviour is a source of guilt feelings.

The feelings that should guide the relationship towards all those people who have *bunkhun* to us, its beneficiaries, are trust, warmth, love, protection, dependence, gratitude, reverence, and acceptance of one's identity. Such profound *bunkhun* relationships are further expressed in the periodic rituals of honouring parents, elders, and teachers as the keystones of the unfailing moral order. Gratitude is also expressed in thanksgiving ritual for a successful harvest.

The complementary opposition of the essentially worldly and female figures of moral goodness and the figures of amoral power, between impotence and might, is further demonstrated by the ideas that guide the division of roles in everyday life. Females are supposed to avoid or shun the manifestations of *saksit* power. They should not touch a Buddha image or a monk, they should stay away from the potent stupas, and should not own powerful amulets or wear sacred tattoos, nor know powerful *khatha*. Women are thought to pollute and neutralize the power of *singsaksit* and are dangerous to the potency of men.[4] The male teacher does not, of course, share in these expectations; but if he is respected for his moral wisdom, people would certainly be surprised to find him equipped with lots of amulets, tattoos, and other protective paraphernalia: he is thought to be already protected by his own moral wisdom, unless, of course, he is a teacher of magic, which is to say, a specialist dealing with *saksit* supernature.[5]

The goodness of Buddhism

The goodness of Buddhism reflects the order of pure virtue that lies beyond the human order of *kilesa* (passion and prejudice) and rebirth *(samsara)*. This pure order represents the realm of truth and the highest *khun*, such as exemplified by the qualities of the Buddha. These are pure virtue *(borisuttikhun)*, the highest compassion *(maha karunathikhun)*, and wisdom *(panyakhun)*. The Buddha is the highest refuge *(sarana)*, and His Teaching *(Dhamma)* directs towards liberation from the fetters of *samsaric* existence; the Noble Eightfold Path leads towards that liberation. This Buddhist Path is essentially a way of morality and wisdom that is indifferent to whatever is *saksit*. Its message is focused beyond the human order, not domesticated as it were, and its way needs to be cultivated in the individual.

Buddhism is not a supernatural manifestation of goodness—although the Buddha as a person is sometimes seen as such—but is rather a path that cultivates goodness and morality as instruments leading to wisdom, equanimity, and ultimately to liberation. The gift of Buddhism is like the gift of the mother or the teacher, a benevolence that does not require any return, and as such it is exemplary of the symbols of goodness in this world. Yet, for all its beneficence, Buddhism does not promise forgiveness and mercy, but places the burden of moral behaviour squarely on the shoulders of the individual, each and every one of whom remains subject to the impersonal law of Karma. Salvation is not a gift but a task, and the Buddhist Path is merely suggesting how to go about it. No wonder that in everyday life the highly tangible figures of mother and teacher remain the very centres of goodness, because they directly help and guide the individual.

The common understanding and practice of Buddhism remains animistic in the sense that merit-making is generally understood as a mechanism to ensure safety and auspiciousness, and thus the institutionalized Buddhism of the masses has become a powerhouse for individual and communal protection. Some people, though, are genuinely interested in following the morality and wisdom of the Buddhist Path and, especially in old age, many practise seriously; such people are no longer interested in the *decha* dimension of existence. To most Thais, however, accruing merit is a technique to ensure safety in a world that is replete with unreliable forces, and the consequent understanding and practice of Buddhism can best be described as 'Buddhist Animism' (Terwiel, 1975).

Interpenetration of *decha* and *khuna*

The interpenetration of the realms of power and moral goodness is embodied in the role of the 'good leader', who is expected to know his way around in both. Such a leader symbolizes, and should personify, goodness and reliability, but also masculinity. This ambiguity is clear in the incumbent role expectations for the father, the headman, the elder, the reliable patron, and ultimately the king. All these should combine benevolence and authority; this duality, however, does not appear to culminate in a central cosmological representation that fuses existential contradictions.

The clearest representation of the interpenetration of power and goodness is in the Sukhothai era ideal of the king as a 'father of the people', or in modern times as a *thamma-racha*, a just king. When the king, under the influence of the 'Khmerization' of Ayutthayan times, came to be perceived as a *thewa-rat*, a Lord of Life, he became clearly identified with the realm of *saksit* power; nowadays the moral imperatives of kingship are strongly emphasized once again. The power and morality of King, Religion and Nation are celebrated in the 'civic religion', along with its identity bestowing symbols, whose centre is in the here-and-now; and is not represented as a cosmic or supernatural principle. The hub of the contemporary Thai cosmos, if there is one, would of necessity be of this world.

Ritually, this civic religion is most clearly expressed in Brahmanic state ceremonials that are intended to ensure the continuity and prosperity of the nation, coordinating the country with the cosmic forces of auspiciousness and the blessings of the *thewada*. Its functioning, like animism, is highly mechanical and incorporates all the symbols of auspiciousness, whether Brahmanic, Buddhist, or animistic in origin. The cast of mind that inspires it is essentially animistic, having safety within the tenuous order of *saksit* and chaotic forces as its goal.

At the level of the small community, the moral unity of the group is still expressed in the rapidly eroding worship of the collective ancestor spirit *(phi pu-ya-ta-yai)* that still exercises a mild social control in parts of the Thai countryside. This depersonalized collectivity of spirits is the guardian of tradition as a moral way of life, and becomes upset over infractions of the rules of social harmony, such as illicit sexual relationships. Nowadays, this collectivity constitutes a minor guardian spirit that can be satisfied by simple ritual which imparts the information that 'all is well'. The ancestors' role in protecting the moral relationship that should exist between all those linked by the bonds of communality is still expressed in marriage and some other life-cycle rituals.

Other ancient ritual enactments, that still persist from the times when the Thai were full-fledged animists, are the *khwan* ('life essence') ceremonies to facilitate the incorporation into the community of strangers, of members who have ventured outside and been in danger, and of members who are in some transitory stage of their life cycle—for instance, marrying, or ordaining as a monk. It is no wonder that these primeval ritual expressions to ensure continuity and auspiciousness have acquired Brahmanic elaborations.

Reflections

Human experience is characterized by basic dualities that can be formulated as complementarities, oppositions, or contradictions, but that nonetheless all belong to the totality of man's state. There are always 'we versus they' situations, insiders versus outsiders, enemies contrasted to friends, trusted intimates and distant strangers, power and powerlessness, order and chaos, safety and danger, and other opposites without end. Within our own experience, we recognize and classify accordingly. Naturally, every philosophy of life, whether of religious inspiration or not, needs to come to grips with these basic dualities and to give them symbolic expressions.

In Thai thinking, the sophisticated elegance of a universal principle combines with the primordial directness of the animistic outlook; somehow Theravada Buddhism and the pre-Buddhist animistic heritage have collaborated in an enduringly harmonious marriage. The Buddhist message does not endow this universe with a comforting centre, but characterizes worldly and cosmic existence as impermanence, suffering, and non-self, imbued with the impersonal principle of Karma. For the contemporary Thai, the pleasant prospect of a heaven peopled by ancestors has been replaced by a long cycle of rebirths, and the knowledge that to do good improves one's karmic position, and that to do evil worsens it. The tribal centre of 'insiders' is somewhat diminished by the introduction of these universal Buddhist principles, but otherwise Buddhist thinking about this life and the universe does not conflict with original animistic cosmology, since both are convincing religious representations of the experience of everyday life.

Thai thinking does not attempt to resolve the contradictory, opposed, or complementary experiences of daily existence, but leaves them side by side just as they are: contradictory, opposed, and complementary as they come to us day by day. Yet, in order to assess (and deal with) the problems of existence in an acceptably optimistic perspective, moral 'inside' classifications versus power-related 'outside' ones have remained quite strong, though not all-pervasive, with the most basic of these considered as 'being safe', in opposition to 'being in danger'. These two complementary experiences are equally integral parts of life.

Ultimately, life is conditioned by the law of Karma, and the only way to overcome this *samsaric* cycle of birth-death-rebirth is to overcome karmic conditioning by the cultivation of morality and wisdom, so escaping from this impermanent and illusory existence into a sphere that is not of this world, and about which we have no knowledge. There is no lasting centre to our world other than the individual person, and there is no cosmic equilibrium of contradictory principles beyond each person's balance of karma. This Buddhist thinking comes very close to explaining existential experience in a convincing perspective, and because Buddhism shares this quality with the very existential explanations of animism, which it does not contradict, the two can exist together, explaining the same reality by similar logic but from a different viewpoint; this at least seems to be the case in Theravada societies.

One of the basic characteristics that Thai animism shares with Theravada Buddhism is the recognition of impermanence, instability, and insecurity, at least in the outside world. The animist recognizes that his life passes among all kinds of unpredictable forces that he needs to find some accommodation with in order to create temporary order. He achieves this by ritual, and by employing a wide range of talismans.

To the animist, the centre of the world is his group, and that centre ensures continuity, stability, and safety. His order lies close to home, the outside being chaotic and capricious, and he only takes the trouble to subject aspects of the outside to temporary order as the need arises. The inside and the outside remain distinct, and the animist's notions of order and disorder—and the means to deal with them—remain distinct, too. This schism being a fundamental attribute of the human experience, it is no cause for surprise that this bifurcation has been elaborated into separate institutionalized religious complexes that can easily coexist. This division is nothing other than an institutionalized reflection of the complexity of experience. The point left to ponder is why other religious thinking has sought to transcend, or at least unify, the basic dualities of existence by suppositions of a single god or a principle of cosmic equilibrium.

In the Thai frame of mind, animistic expression, 'magic', and popular Buddhism deal essentially with the tenuous order of *saksit*, plus the chaotic realm of evil powers, and these religious expressions should be understood as one complex. Brahmanic expressions (including state ritual, civic religion, and *khwan* ceremonies) are essentially concerned with the continuity of the group and auspiciousness in a hazardous environment; such expressions are directed toward mediation between the moral inside and the amoral outside.

Khuna (moral goodness)

Order	Pure order	Order of goodness
Symbol	The Buddha (Dhamma; Sangha)	The mother (parents; teacher)
Quality	Pure virtue Pure compassion Wisdom Stillness Stability	Moral goodness (pure *bunkhun*) Reliability Forgiveness
Time perspective	Cycle of rebirth	Continuity
Religious complex	Doctrinal Buddhism Eight-fold Path	To honour parents, elders and teachers Cult of *Mae Phosop*
Aim	Liberation; better rebirth	Moral continuity; identity; fertility
Means	To make merit as a moral pursuit	To acknowledge *khun*; to be grateful; to return favours Agricultural ritual
Infraction	Sin; activates	Karmic retribution; feelings of guilt
Direction	Ultimate refuge	One receives first

Interpenetration		Decha (power)
Order of community	Tenuous order	Chaos
The 'good' leader (*thamma-racha*; 'father')	*Saksit* forces (spirits; *thewada*)	Bad spirits (death)
Phra-khuna and *phra-decha* Safety Mutuality Stability to be defended	Ambiguous: potentially protective; benevolent yet jealous; amoral Instability	Entirely dangerous; whimsical; threatening Immoral Capriciousness
		Immediate
Lifelong	Short time	
		Magic (mobilizing *saksit* power)
Brahmanic ritual; ancestor cult; *khwan* ceremonies 'Civic religion'	Animistic ritual (including popular Buddhism)	*Awa-mongkhon* (death) ritual
Auspiciousness; continuity and safety; peace	To ensure protection and good fortune	To ward off danger
To be a dependable and reliable group member; to respect tradition	To show respect; to vow and redeem the vow To make merit as a protective pursuit	Protective amulets, *khatha*, etc. Powerful magic. To make merit for the deceased
Stupidity; social sanctions;	**activates** revenge; bad fortune loss of face;	Activates danger
Reciprocity	One has to give/respect first	One is extorted

These latter expressions serve to ensure and sustain auspiciousness, and thus they are, apart from calendrical and life-cycle rituals, most typically manifested in astrological calculation.

The cult of the order of goodness enjoys little overt religious expression, but is tangibly expressed in the mother-centred ideology that teaches dependence on parents, elders, teachers, and on tradition—the obligation of the younger generation to recognize the *bunkhun* of the older generation. Respect for the order of goodness is most strongly reinforced by the feelings of guilt and the social and karmatic consequences attendant on the sin of *nerakhun*—the failure to recognize the obligations of gratitude. The cult of goodness is also propagated in the rituals directed to *Mae Phosop* and *Mae Thorani*.

The quest for salvation is expressed in the earnest following of the Buddhist Path and is generally a preoccupation of old age; this self-centred quest turns its back on the vicissitudes and onuses of daily life. While symbolically beneficial to the stability of the group, the Buddhist quest for merit in old age should not be equated with the popular merit-making practices to gain safety and protection. Everyday merit-making is offered in the hope of a rather immediate return, whereas in old age, Buddhist practice tends to be a quest to realize the hope for a better rebirth and for liberation, the aim being less to 'buy' protection for oneself than to hold devoutly to the practice of morality as a refuge leading to ultimate rewards.

This recognition of various realms of experience is reflected institutionally in a similar variety of religious complexes. The acknowledgment of a multifarious cosmos would seem to be closer to life's reality than is a reduction of everything into one integrated concept to explain the often contradictory experiences of life. Because the postulate of Karma easily accomplishes this, and since Buddhism recognizes and explains Dharma as a broad stream that encompasses life in all its variety, the Thais have no difficulty in calling themselves or their world 'Buddhist'.

Timeliness of Thai symbolic representations

To be without land—or to lose it—was formerly an exceptional situation, but at present such deprivation has become quite normal. The purchasing power of the baht erodes day by day. The reasonable expectation that education leads to respectable employment is contradicted by experience. The modern world is diffused with increasingly rapid change and a self-seeking, impersonal 'system' that causes feelings of powerlessness for most. No wonder that the old animistic perceptions of power are being strongly revitalized in a process where the force of money is often felt to be immoral and nondomesticated; the impersonal and difficult-to-control power of money has now begun to dominate the more personal and addressable bonds of yester-year. Patron-client relationships have been replaced or subverted by businesslike ties, and often the experience of power is that of anonymous compulsion.

Consequently, we witness a strong revival of animistic expressions. According to the research of Peltier, the number of magically gifted *luang pho* monks famous for protective amulets has increased spectacularly over the past forty or so years. Trouble at borders has increased the amount of danger and subsequently the demand for amulets. *Pluk phra* ceremonial that was relatively infrequent a few decades ago is now conducted at two or three-year intervals at the major temples.[6] Certain shrines, such as the one for the Four-faced Brahma at the Erawan Hotel, enjoy a steadily increasing popularity at this time when modern influences are eroding expectations of stability. Also among modern people the old perception of power as an amoral or immoral force is strengthened by the experience of disorder and insecurity. In brief, Thai animistic perceptions are strengthened and validated by the experiences of modernity, and are still very timely.

The experience of contemporary life corresponds to the old concept of amoral power in Thai culture, but is that experience desirable? Is impersonal power legitimate in any way? Many Thais doubt this and some alternatives to this problem have been formulated over the past sixty years.

The oldest alternative is the quest for the legitimation of the exercise of power in the 'public' world through constitutionalism and democracy, which can be interpreted as the spreading and sharing of power, of placing power under the moral control of all citizens. However, sixteen constitutions and sixty years of discussion have not much changed the exercise of power and have contributed little to the realization of effective popular control; one reason for this failure is that the ideal of a moral system surrounding and controlling power goes against the grain of a hierarchical society and its culture. One may see the attempts to establish democracy as, at best, attempts to mediate between morality and the powerful areas of existence (chapter 9).

The other alternative involves propagating the Buddhist Path as a solution for all worldly problems, the idea being that if the Thais profess to be Buddhists then they should be true Buddhists and organize their personal lives and society accordingly (chapter 8). This perspective is, of course, highly utopian and very much in contradiction with the animistic perception of existence. Moral goodness certainly has its laws but so does power, and each needs to be lived and dealt with on its own terms.

INTERPRETING ACTION: REFLECTIONS ON PRESENTATION AND POWER

Approaches to the interpretation of Thai behaviour and action

Observers of social life in Thailand have for long been intrigued by the apparent cleavage that seems to characterize Thai behaviour. Although almost nobody disputes such observations, social thinkers have so far failed to place them in a meaningful indigenous perspective, that is, to interpret them in their cultural context.

The oldest sociological interpretation of Thai social intercourse was formulated by those who see Thailand as a 'loosely structured' social system. They noted a paucity of institutional arrangements and an intriguing amount of individualism. The 'loose structure' analysis has been brought to its logical conclusion by Phillips (1965): the Thais are self-seeking individualists and social life unfolds as a kind of stage play where individuals hide their intentions and feelings behind a 'social cosmetic' of politeness and smiles. This picture of an individual-centred society logically painted a highly unpredictable social process characterized by a short time perspective, pragmatic social arrangements, and inter-individual uncertainty. Steven Piker (1975) and Adul Wichiencharoen (1976) seem to expound this view and also to draw a line, interpreting the individual to be on one side and the social process on the other.

These 'loose structure' interpretations inevitably fail to explain the undeniable institutional continuity of Thai society through centuries to the present, and Thai critics of the concept have hypothesized more acceptable theories to explain the different types of Thai social interaction. According to Boonsanong Punyodyana (1969), a society needs institutional continuity;

and Thai society, like any other, is characterized by a continuity of the institutions that shape and require predictable and stable behaviour. Next to predictable institutional behaviour, he posits an interpersonal level of behaviour where individuals are free to act according to their own norms and wishes, that being the loosely structured sphere of Thai social behaviour.

Titaya Suvanajata (1976) seems to invert Boonsanong's line of thinking; on the one hand he notes formal relationships that are dyadic (paired), voluntary, and ritualistic—or outward directed; these relationships are not motivated by long term obligation or deep psychological investment. On the other hand he notes closed-personal relationships that are informed by *bunkhun* and a deep sense of obligation; these relationships would be enduring, stable and reliable.

It is of interest to note that Boonsanong and Titaya seem to draw the line between types of interaction at more or less the same point, yet they differ radically in interpretation, Boonsanong being oriented more towards western theory and Titaya taking more of a Thai observer's point of view. Both recognize a cleavage in Thai interaction and it seems that recognition of this dichotomy is crucial to understanding Thai social life. Titaya's ideas have the merit of introducing the feeling of commitment and obligation that is invested in one type of relationship or the other, as the distinguishing variable.

Consequently it seems valid to doubt whether the foreign concepts of formal, interpersonal, and institutional relationships are meaningful in describing Thai interaction. A *bunkhun* relationship cannot always be classified as either formal or informal. Such a relationship may simultaneously be interpersonal and institutionalized. A relationship with a patron may be both highly interpersonal and highly formal. Similarly, Phillips's notion of social cosmetic covers areas of behaviour that are difficult to describe as formal in ordinary village interaction. What is apparently needed is a different system of classification with criteria that are hand-tailored to the Thai situation and that answer the questions "How does ego perceive?", "How does ego classify?", and "How does ego feel?" first of all.

Titaya classifies types of relationships according to the quantity and the quality of the *bunkhun* involved, that *bunkhun* presumably fading out toward the far end of the scale where behaviour becomes purely transactional and socio-psychologically neutral (such as in buying and selling from strangers). This classificatory system fits with the idea that Thai relationships are primarily person-centred and only to a lesser degree institutionally defined. This person-centredness is, of course, not indicative of the so-called individualism that is often attributed to Thai motivations.

According to Weerayudh Wichiarajote, the deeper foundation of personally motivated relationships lies with a need for affiliation that is based not on individualism but rather on low self-confidence. His and Titaya's observations strengthen each other: Thai relationships build on personal motivations, based on *bunkhun* and obligation, on the need for affiliation and security, and the more intense these motivations, the more stable and predictable the relationship will be. One should be loyal to one's parents, relatives, circle of friends, and classmates; the further one moves into the realm of outsiders, the less predictable relationships will be.

An essential difference between Titaya's and Weerayudh's interpretations is located in the foundation of relationships. Titaya's keystone is *bunkhun*, which implies the presence or absence of a moral element in the relationship. Weerayudh's psychologically inspired need for affiliation is morally neutral and applies to all relationships, whether motivated by gratefulness and obligation or by considerations of power, patronage and protection.

All works dealing with Thai politics and administration emphasize the importance of the struggle for power. Relationships and associations among non-intimates seem to be inspired by the need for power, self-aggrandizement, acceptance, patronage and protection. How power operates has so far best been described by Riggs (1966), while Hanks (1962) has been the first to draw attention to the cultural underpinnings of Thai action in moral and power perspectives.

Interpreting the analyses of Thai values as presented by Thai sociologists, such as Phaithun Khruakeo (1969), Suphatra Suphap (1975), Phaibun Chang-rian (1973), and Anon Aphaphirom (1974), one is struck by the emphasis on categories of power and the need for social acceptance and recognition. To none of these writers does loose structure or individualism appear to be highly significant, all of them emphasizing wealth, power, authority, rank and status as the deepest motivations and ultimate goals. While they modify this value structure somewhat when discussing life in the countryside, it is still striving for power, rank, and recognition that best explains the dynamics of interpersonal relationships, the condition of having power or not being the most basic principle of classification.

In the following analysis we shall seek our way through these various interpretations of the observable types of Thai behaviour and interaction. In doing so we shall investigate whether the ideas contained in the symbolic representations help to elucidate the practical world view and everyday life classifications. The point of concentration of this chapter will be with the perception of interaction with persons who are not intimate, who are relatively distant, and about whom expectations are uncertain; the next chapter will concentrate on the relationships with near persons.

Reflections on presentation in everyday life

Thai society values smooth interaction and the avoidance of overt conflict; when everybody knows his place and behaves accordingly, these ideals can be achieved. In everyday life this is induced by appropriate polite behaviour that is expressed in befitting presentation. Smiles and polite speech facilitate the interaction in which individuals somehow flow past each other without hindrance or obstacle. This smoothness is often accompanied by genuine kindness and an interest in the well-being of the other. Such interaction both demands a show of kindness and encourages it. If the other party is contented, he will be harmless and kind in return, and all can feel at ease and mutually ingratiated.

This kindness and concern (e.g., "Have you eaten yet or not, sir?") does not go deep and is no sign of commitment. When a market woman sells her limes four to the baht, and she decides to add a fifth as an extra, then she has been kind to me and both of us will feel pleased because of her kindness. Yet there is no commitment on her side to give me another five on my next purchase, nor am I committed to buy all my limes from her in the future—although she may hope so ("Please come back and support me again, sir"). What has been created is smooth and pleasant interaction as a purpose unto itself, as an expression of the Thai ethos, of a tone of life that seeks a peaceful and pleasant atmosphere.

Contrarily, it is disturbing, and sometimes even a frightening experience when people fail to smile and merely show a stern face. In such situations one feels insecure, anticipating trouble, because the atmosphere of smoothness seems to be corrupted by ulterior, threatening motives.

While presentation of self is a primary means to keep interaction kind and pleasant, presentation also keeps individuals distanced from each other because of the implicit expectation that the surface also is the essence of social reality. Consequently, the art of role-playing is highly developed and, essential for the success of the social show. The inferior little guy *(phunoi)* approaches the superior big man *(phuyai)* with a respectful greeting gesture *(wai)* that is reciprocated according to hierarchical expectations. When unfamiliar laymen are near, the monk will adjust his robe; the policeman in uniform may smoke and be arrogant but, as a representative of power, he should not show intimacy and preferably refrain from smiling; the seller of goods, on the other hand, puts on a smile to show that he can be trusted. Upon meeting, one should smile and people are expected to dress according to station in life (eventually with coat and necktie!), because presentation expresses the social persona and claim to status.

It takes but little time observing Thai behaviour to become adept at perceiving who is superior and who is inferior. The presentation of self tends to include displaying the whole set of one's social arsenal, and such assets should not be hidden. Even in the most casual encounters, people probe to discover the other person's social rank and, consequently, their relative social distance. What work does he do? To what groups does he belong? What position does he hold? Is he rich or poor? Has he studied and where? His age, his relatives, his group, and his income: all this should be known so that both parties can place each other accordingly. Smoothness is then expected to result, the right language can be chosen, and everybody will be at ease.

The Thai social process does deal not so much with distinct individual personalities on their own merit as with ranks and status positions, and consequently it is untypical and even foolish to hide behind modesty when one is entitled to honour. Symbols of status should be displayed and people should live up to them. Status has its own social obligations and often requires the showing of benevolence and generosity. Because most participants in any situation will be keenly aware of relative hierarchy, it is loathsome to exert or press one's position and cause other people to feel slighted or repressed, particularly when the inferior has already politely and subtly indicated his lower position. As long as the atmosphere of friendliness dominates, status and hierarchy will be accepted and appreciated.

In ordinary life people prefer to take pleasant or, at the very least, polite presentation for social reality. That convention, however, means more than the enactment of non-committal kindness and unequal mutuality. In presentation, the expectations of society and the individual meet. Consequently, it calls for heavy investment in both smooth interaction and in the projection of prestige and dignity. This investment is not simply an investment in cosmetics (Phillips, 1965:66) to keep interactions free of trouble and hierarchically clear; the value of presentation is also extremely psychological, serving the feelings of identity and acceptance.

Among non-intimate persons the mutual determination of status hinges primarily on the recognition of relative power. Respect naturally flows to power, and people like to be respected. As soon, therefore, as one enters into the Thai game of the display of power, one has entered into the game of rank, respect and honour, and concern for presentation of self. In this light, the observations of the Thai sociologists begin to make sense. According to them, the primary Thai values are wealth, power, seniority, rank, and being the boss, all of these values being intensely other-directed referents that are irrelevant in the more relaxed association with intimates.

It is small wonder that, as one's hierarchical position rises, the investment in presentation also increases. People build up stature by increasing their resources—and by the demonstration of them. Since Thailand has become a relatively open society, in which the monopoly of the old nobility has been broken, the competition for power and status has become even more intense, such as demonstrated by the flagrant display of status symbols and the blatant show-offs that fill the society pages of the newspapers.

Among polite persons it is believed that power should not be coarsely presented, but rather in a pleasant, smiling, and self-confident manner. However, many people appear to be vulnerable and are easily insulted if not shown what they consider to be appropriate honour and respect. Persons who feel slighted may turn vengeful, and seeking revenge for a perceived insult is highly endemic; such vindictiveness is demonstrated by gory stories in the daily newspaper and the rich vocabulary to express hatred and revenge.

In summation, Thailand is a society of rather conservative people who appreciate the predictability and quietness—the security—of a well-ordered *(riaproi)* social life to which they willingly conform; as long as people honour its rules, there is room for some tolerated individual deviation. In interaction with non-intimate persons, people most often perceive each other as potentially harmful, because real intentions are often kept hidden. Consequently, strangers and superiors need to be placated by polite and pleasant behaviour. The ritual smile and appropriate presentation often hide insecurity and anxiety. Role-playing and maintaining the external appearance of an orderly relationship are the primary defense mechanisms and the best techniques for both controlling and masking that insecurity and anxiety. Thus presentation becomes deeply important, both socially and psychologically; as consciousness and demonstration of good manners it is the treasure of those who take their social appearance seriously.[1]

The image that Thai society often projects at first impression, The land of Smiles, is a reflection of the acceptance of the reality of presentation and the incumbent maintenance of pleasantness, even under adverse conditions. Such pleasantness is often genuine, but it also hides pressures, both socio-psychological and individual. In the following sections we shall investigate the extent to which the Thai ethos and the perception of non-intimates may contribute to the pressures and problems of contemporary social life.

Consequences of the perception of non-intimate distant others

From a survey of 130,000 young Thais, the psychiatrist Udomsilp Srisaengnam (1977) reached the conclusion that twenty-five percent of the population between twenty-five and thirty years succumb to some form of neurosis because of the impact of modernity and tension of conflicting values. Research by Chira Sitasuwan et al. (1976) in Bangkok Noi District sampled a section of those married, and found that fifty percent were not in good mental health.[2] Although this figure appears high when compared to the ten percent rate of mental disturbance for the population of developing countries as a whole (as estimated by the World Health Organization), it is not unlikely that Thai society generates culturally unique psychological tensions by repressing individuals through identifying them with their presentation, thus stifling their needs for self-expression and open communication.

In the admittedly very violent year 1976, the police statistics recorded the impressive murder rate of 0.3 to thousand denizens, but, according to police officials, that figure probably needed to be multiplied by two since people, especially in the countryside, are not eager to add insult to injury by involving the authorities in their political, business, and private squabbles. In 1994, the prisons harboured 107,000 inmates, which yields the top rating of 1.8 per thousand of the population. Petty crime and violence are endemic. The number of prostitutes is estimated to approximate one percent of the population, while drug addiction has grown to become one of the country's major problems. Moreover, corruption and abuse of power seem to be the normal practices of the day.

A key to understanding such facts may proceed from a deeper reflection about the Thai perception of non-intimate distant others. If such persons are perceived as potentially harmful, then it is wise to maintain distance and encourage an atmosphere of fluidity while avoiding involvement in each other's problems. This practice may alienate and disorient all those who have a high need for sociability. Apart from mental health problems, some may seek self-expression in a subculture, others revert to criminal practices, or may demonstrate deviant behaviour. Many turn to drugs and liquor. These, and other reactions to the problems of interpersonal distance and of the personality repression that follows from the demand to identify with role and status, are currently exacerbated by the experience of urban anonymity.

Other people, who have no problem in adjusting, are frustrated because they do not feel respected. Since they also have invested in their dignity, at least according to their means and social place, they expect to be taken seriously, and not to be treated as a nullity. Yet there are strong tendencies to treat the lesser person arrogantly, causing him to feel oppressed and pushed around. Such purely negative feelings are a result of what is basically an insult to the minor person who has no redress but to feel disrespected and stifled.

Because this sort of treatment is by no means rare, it may partly help explain the quest for diplomas, government employment, or even a position in the monkhood. After all, a Buddhist monk *(phra)*, generally of the most humble origins, merits and receives honour by the fact of his ordination, and by thus occupying a position that should be respected. Moreover, he is also thought to be associated with religious or white magical *saksit* power.

Other people choose to follow a different way to social self-validation, and seek power that inspires fear rather than respect; in daily life it is recommended to avoid them or to buy them off. Before elaborating on the role of the blatant hooligan or the more subtle example of the corrupt civil servant, let us see what happens if an otherwise pleasant person discards his nice presentation and suddenly shows himself as a threat.

The prime example is the drunk, the man who has temporarily lost control of himself and no longer conforms to the requirements of his status. Excessive drinking is an accepted foible in which one often shows oneself to be a cowboy, a he-man, who demonstrates his machismo and hidden power. Yet some men who get drunk become quite terrible, forgetting their pleasant presentation, while giving free rein to hidden and frightening emotions.

The Thai reaction to this naked emotion is to be extremely circumspect, tolerant and outwardly friendly. People endlessly try to soothe and appease the drunk, addressing him politely as older brother or uncle, submitting to his wishes but generally altogether failing to placate the aggressive power that has been unleashed by the spirit of alcohol. If calamity is avoided, the next day everybody seems to have forgotten, and the malefactor is obviously not held responsible for his behaviour the night before.

It could be very dangerous to eject the drunk by strong words or violence. After all, he might return with a gun and start a shoot-out to avenge his insulted ego. Another similar, oft-repeated situation is where absolute strangers commit no offense beyond staring at each other, without smiling, when one party suddenly picks up his symbol of masculinity and riddles the staring person with bullets. He feels as if his presentation has been pierced by the staring of the other, which is not only an intrusion, but also threatening and insulting, thus calling out for revenge.

Generally, people fear and avoid confrontation. Showing respect and friendliness—and, even more, submission—is therefore best and the only mechanism of defense for those who are without power. Interestingly, these are precisely the necessary and sufficient strategies to interact successfully with distant persons. Such persons may be seen as occupying relative positions of power that each of them wants to see respected and recognized. To institute that recognition, respect should be shown, ranging from a polite smile to an elaborate ceremony honouring the superior. Then the superior's power is supposed to be neutralized and harmless, possibly even benevolent and protective. This behaviour need not go further than show indeed, and there is no harm in making obeisance to, then subsequently taking advantage of power; on the contrary, such behaviour is widely admired, the folk heroes *Khun Phaen* and *Sithanonchai* providing prime examples.

Certain types of people are fully identified with malicious power, such as the roughnecks or hoodlums *(naklaeng)*; they do not bother to present themselves politely but openly demonstrate their contempt for others in behaviour and vocabulary. In this category we also find civil servants who do not trouble to hide their intentions behind smiles but who make their desires immediately known, unbashfully and unashamed. They inspire fear, and crossing their path inevitably means hardship. As persons they seem to have totally divorced their behaviour towards their intimates from their public roles towards distant persons.

This thinking on role-playing provides us with an interesting perspective on the widespread popularity of prostitution. To sell one's body to non-intimate distant persons is merely relating to the world outside and does not imply any feelings of loyalty or respect. Buying or selling sex is a monetary transaction like any other, and money is widely admired. Neither party is personally involved; it is simply a business transaction in which the loss-of-face element is amply compensated by money. To be the minor wife *(mianoi)* or mistress of a rich man is to be under his patronage, and his status, power and wealth reflect on her. It is an honourable, much sought-after status, particularly for women of a distinctly lower social level.

Descending the scale of status, money and power, the profession of selling one's body is delineated by an extensive hierarchical vocabulary reflected in recent legal deliberations about where to draw the line between prostitutes and the more noble butterflies. The inmates of a brothel and streetwalkers would probably be classified as prostitutes, but as soon as the girl seeks her clients in a bar, a coffee shop, or a massage parlour, she may consider herself to be in a different category. (I am not aware of whether the venerable law-makers ever deliberated the problem of mistresses and minor wives, but it is of interest to note that no one less than King Rama VI once devoted an article to this institution).

The way of the prostitutes is a way to cope with survival in Thai society and to face its realities. Prostitutes cash in on the ambiguous cultural values of prestige, power and money. There is nothing wrong in prostituting oneself when it results in money or powerful protection. As long as a woman cares for her relatives and recompenses the *bunkhun* of her parents with gifts and money, she can still see—and present—herself as a good person. When she has accumulated enough or when her fortunes turn, she may return to her village of origin to marry and be accepted with little or no stigma.

In a subtle way the corrupt government official falls precisely between the positions of the monk and the prostitute. He occupies a position that should be respected, yet seeks money as the recognition of his status. He is very willful or thick-faced and wants his power to be taken seriously; he is as dangerous as any *naklaeng* or spirit that is not respected and bought off.

In the modern world of urban anonymity people have to fight their own battles. The measure of that world is money and there are few mutually accepted moral guidelines. Alliances with power are pragmatically inspired and consequently a negative, selfish form of rampant individualism *(tua-khrai-tua-man)* may dominate the scene and inspire lawlessness, excessive exploitation, profiteering, and the widespread practice of corruption. When money and power dominate social intercourse, society may easily become a jungle where one only cares for oneself, one's intimates and group; such unfortunate tendencies are certainly strong and increasing in present Thai social life, both because of its own cultural heritage and because of modern influences.

Social psychological hypotheses

Power is at once desirable and dangerous. Because one cannot escape from its influence, one needs to deal with it; this realization informs the perception of and behaviour towards non-intimate distant persons. Contemplating the consequences that the perception of distant persons may have in Thai social psychology, we may hypothesize that several personality characteristics are fairly common.

Some people invest heavily in and identify almost totally with their social 'face'; they are consequently highly vulnerable in their presentation. Anxiety and insecurity about status would therefore seem to be endemic, provoking feelings of inferiority in some people or a desire for revenge and vindication. The element of power is thus very important but also potentially dangerous, and we may, therefore, expect submerged feelings of suspicion and fear, alongside the resultant techniques to avoid confrontations.

The internalized, almost reflexive attitudes of avoidance, non-commitment, and a superficial show of respect generate feelings of non-responsibility towards other persons and towards the social process at large, leading to superficiality and fluidity of contacts, emotional distance between persons, *choei* (indifference) and *chaiyen* (self-control) attitudes. These attitudes also contribute to the wise course of taking things as they come, entertaining a short time perspective, and becoming aware of the vicissitudes of life. Being apprehensive also stimulates the tendency to look for the enjoyable and amusing *(sanuk)* side of life. The pleasant surface of things is best treated as their reality, and to get involved is disturbing and dangerous; so let it be, because after all it is just the outside, a game, a show. Those who believe only in that show and who deeply involve themselves in it are most often characterized by strong social ambition, and they are prototypes of the drive for power. Those who are without power or ambition will cultivate attitudes of indifference and resignation; they do not so much feel involved as manipulated, exploited, and subservient in their contacts with the powerful world outside the home.

Conclusion

These reflections on presentation and power have not done full justice to the intricate and fascinating problem of interaction with distant persons. Moreover, to achieve some perspective, the interaction with near persons should also be analyzed (see following chapter). In conclusion, though, we may propose that presentation is one's self-portrayal to the outside, to the world of power; presentation seeks prestige and requires a psychological investment.

In the social sphere one is vulnerable and needs to be careful. Presentation is a kind of projected ego that will be judged by non-intimate persons beyond the home. Presentation defines one's social persona and how one is measured, more in terms of conformity and power than of knowledge, integrity, or morality. It is the world of make-believe in which for many people a great deal of emotion has been invested: when that image is attacked, feelings of identity may collapse.

Besides one's presentation to outsiders, we find the near persons with whom one feels to be related and to whom one is good, and here lies one's true self. For most people the relationship with near persons is of the greatest significance, a haven of peace and security in a world that is animated by power and prestige. The deepest self is often a secret about which the individual knows little, although it may erupt as the Nemesis of the insulted 'face'; normally the deep self hides behind a smile, yet sometimes it shows itself, most often driven by uncontrolled feelings of revenge.

The Thai ethos appears to be quite efficient and wise in dealing with a world full of powerful strangers and superiors. It copes with suspicion and fear by avoiding confrontation ("Do not get involved where you have no business"), by constant effort to keep social interactions friendly, smooth and superficial, and by looking for the pleasant side of life. This wisdom is reflected in the concern for a congenial atmosphere and efforts to make others feel at ease. Altogether this gives everyday interaction the flavour of pleasantness and relaxation, of tolerance and non-involvement. It is wise to know one's place and to accept life as it comes. Yet a negative effect is that many individuals may suffer from a lack of self-expression; such frustration is aggravated by the pressure and value conflicts that are generated by modernity.

CHAPTER 4

INTERPRETING ACTION:
REFLECTIONS ON TRUST,
RELAXATION, AND SELF

Social psychological approaches to the interpretation
of Thai behaviour and action

Utilizing a Freudian interpretation of indulgent nurture, Snit Smuckarn has developed the hypothesis that, "Generally speaking, the Thais have a firm belief in themselves and very much like to admire themselves; they trust other people and tend to look at life optimistically; on the other hand they love extravagance, have no discipline, and are ridden by sexual anxiety" (1976a:31–2). In order to strengthen his argument he refers to proponents of the loosely-structured school of interpretation, such as Embree (1950) and Phillips (1965:32–33). In another publication he follows in the steps of many foreigners and adds Buddhist reasons to his argument (1976 b:228–30).

Snit is not alone among Thai observers of Thai society in reaching such interpretations. Adul Wichiencharoen sees the Thais as individualists and self-reliant loners (1976). Khunying Ambhorn Meesook (1973:3) and Suphatra Suphaab (1975:12–3) agree, although their evaluation of Thai individualism is more negative, criticizing the tendency to egoism and social irresponsibility; yet Khunying Ambhorn also interprets this tendency as admirable self-reliance.

Steven Piker (1975) does not disagree, but he is more subtle in his interpretation: the Thais need to rely upon themselves because of the perceived indeterminancy of motives of others and the recognition of a general unreliability of intentions; like many other observers he supports his findings with Buddhist wisdom about the nature of reality and the Buddhist dogma that one must depend on oneself to reach liberation.

Weerayudh Wichiarajote postulates an entirely different picture of society and behaviour. He characterizes Thailand as an affiliative society in which people greatly depend upon each other and thus find their security in dependence and patronage rather than in individualism. According to Sensenig's presentation of Weerayudh's theory,

> The basic drive of individual behaviour is to establish extensive networks of personal relationships: these basic motivational drives are characterized by the need for friendship, love, warmth, and social acceptance. In general, feelings are counted more than reason, and this tends to result in low self-discipline (1975:118–19).

Weerayudh's explanation portrays individualism in a new light. As personality traits he notes low self-discipline, low self-confidence, and low self-respect, all factors that contribute to the observed tendency to seek immediate gratification and a strong desire for affiliation. If these character-istics and drives are as strong as they are sometimes thought to be, dis-appointment, insecurity, frustration, and loneliness must be quite common, leading either to high conformity or to deviance, both of which are readily observable. But with the addition of conformity and deviance, the picture of Thai individualism becomes radically different from the earlier surmised self-confidence.

Weerayudh's observations appear to concur with the cardinal values of Thai society as described by Thai sociologists. These sociologists note social acclaim and status, success and showing off and—by implication—status anxiety as the predominant cultural themes, which leads me to hypothesize other-directedness rather than individual self-sufficiency as a core character-istic. These sociologists also note strong tendencies towards anti-social behaviour. The values that they note are so incompatible with any possible interpretation of Buddhism that they abstain from comment on that subject.

The problem with the first mentioned culture-and-personality and loose-structure approaches is that they try to derive too much from too little evidence, and that their proponents are too eager to make theory work. Mother's milk and indulgence, late weaning and undemanding toilet training, are supposed to promote individualism and self-confidence, which in turn are thought to be supported by Buddhism, further leading to the myth of a loosely structured social system (Mulder, 1969). There are no good reasons why the experience of indulgent nurture and tolerance should not engender high dependence, personal insecurity, doubt, vulnerability, tendencies towards machismo and ostentation—not to speak of a measure of mutual tolerance for deviance.

Moreover, apart from the actual observation of behaviour, we need to search for the cultural input that creates such behaviour. What is taught to children? How is the world presented to them, apart from indulgent nurture? In other words, what is the world view of their parent's generation, and what is presented to children in terms of values, ideas and motives?

The world as presented to the child

It is a truism to observe that children the world over are dependent on their parents and elders; it is quite another thing, however, to investigate the cultural content that is inculcated during that dependence. Dependency combined with indulgence may stimulate deep feelings of dependence and trust. The Thai child is not encouraged to be self-dependent in its childish ways, but rather to depend on others for its satisfaction. Soon it is taught to acknowledge its dependence by respecting its sources (especially the mother) and by developing a sense of obligation. The child reciprocates its dependence by conformity and gratefulness and by not imposing itself as a personality, that is, to remain *choei* (silent, still) and to keep its feelings to itself, which can be interpreted as a form of self-reliance training (Sensenig, 1977:171,178).

The world outside the trusted home is presented as fearsome, threatening and unreliable, populated with spirits, tigers, *thewada*, fate, and other mysterious forces; these forces need to be respected and will seek revenge for infraction of the familial traditions and rules.

What are these rules? The child is soon indoctrinated, first casually, and later on by explicit teaching, that its mother is its everything.

> Your mother loves you more than anybody else. She has given birth to you; you have grown up because of sucking her blood. She has been feeding you and caring for you. She knows what is best for you. You should return her love, be thankful to her, respect her, yet in all your life you will never be able

to repay her for the overflowing goodness she has done for you. Never, never forget to return the goodness that she has given to you; be grateful and fulfil your filial obligation.

This strong emphasis on the goodness *(bunkhun)* of the mother and the respect owed to her position serve a double purpose: it creates a sense of dependence, respect and obligation, feelings of awe *(kreng)* for goodness, and it also incorporates the hopes of the parents to be taken care of in old age. The mother-child relationship is at the heart of the ideology that informs the Thai way of life.

Respect and obedience to elders, trust in their wisdom and protection, the need to return favours received, all these are strong themes in Thai culture. The underlying idea is the principle of mutual dependence and reciprocity, and the principle of being practically and morally indebted. It is the recognition that people need each other if they want to go on with the business of living, formulated in a system of mutual but unequal moral obligations, with due respect for tradition and the wisdom of elders.

The necessary basic attitudes that are instilled at an early age, are *kreng-chai* (combining inhibition and consideration), *krengklua* (awe, respectful fear), *khaorop* and *napthu* (to esteem and to respect), politeness and obedience, recognition of *khun* (goodness that results in obligation), and *katanyu* (gratefulness), beside the fear that mysterious forces will automatically be activated to revenge infractions against parents and elders who are invariably pictured as wise, moral, worthy of respect, and epitomized in the figures of the mother and the *khru* (guru, teacher).

Similar to the mother, the *khru* is also expected to be filled with loving kindness, to be reliable and to represent goodness and morality. But apart from these idealized categories of near persons one should avoid risks and recognize that other people are vulnerable and may seek revenge for infractions against their egos. Children soon learn that they should let sleeping dogs lie, show respect, be willing to accommodate, keep the social process pleasant and non-controversial, and understand that disturbance may be dangerous.

As long as one toes the line there is no reason for fear, and the obligations of reverence and respect are not burdensome. On the contrary, they reflect comfort in dependence and are a sign of reliability, continuity, and acceptance. People are made to feel dependent and to value their refuges, not so much having a firm belief in their own personality as a belief in their group and havens *(thiphung)*. As long as a child grows up, it depends on the goodness of others. Soon it learns to reciprocate, first by being grateful and by showing recognition, and then, later in life, by extending *bunkhun* towards other persons who are expected to be grateful in turn. This mechanism of obligation and reciprocity cements groups, first of all the family, then the community, and further, personally specific associations; such alliances lead to the attitude 'my group, right or wrong' *(phuak-khrai phuak-man)*. These groups, from moral to functional, comprise one's moral order and are one's refuges in an unreliable world.

Hierarchy versus trust

The world as presented to the child reflects the world view of its parental generation and has three basic dimensions: inside, outside, and hierarchy. The inside is the world of near persons, of home, family, and community; the outside is the world of distant persons, of strangers, power, and suspicion. Both realms indisputably have their hierarchy. Where hierarchical relationships are understood to mean the recognition of wisdom, leadership, benevolence and relative age, we may call it the hierarchy of unequal moral relationships characteristic of the inside world. Outside of these family-type relationships, hierarchy is primarily characterized by the element of unequal power. I do not wish to dispute that the inside-outside patterns of behaviour and social practice overlap and melt into each other: they do, but there are important differences in the psychological or emotional components of the two situations, the inside being 'natural' and informed by benevolence, trust and protection, while the outside is informed by the power to rule, to compel, and to relish. A father is expected to be good, to have *bunkhun* towards his dependents, and he does not need to be paid for that; a hierarchical superior may be good, but generally needs to be honoured or to be bribed to be good. While father is expected to be constantly reliable, an outsider is only temporarily trustworthy.

Interaction with intimates is inspired by consideration *(krengchai)* and, at its most intimate levels, by a feeling of mutual understanding *(khwam khao-kan-dai)* and cordial relaxation *(khwam pen kan-eng)*. The Thai ethos of friendliness and kindness that appeared to have a self-defence function in interaction with distant persons also pertains to near-person interaction, but here its psychological and sociological significance is different. To avoid overt conflict with powerful outsiders is only wise, but to avoid conflict with intimates is more than wise: it is also pleasant and rewarding. To present a smile to a distant person neutralizes his potential harm, while to smile to an intimate is an expression of good humour, trust or benevolence; to show respect to a superior is a technique to be safe, to show respect to an elder is to acknowledge his benevolence and expresses one's gratitude. Similarly, to nurture quiet and orderly relationships among intimates is like caring for one's home; maintaining complaisant relationships with outsiders is rather inspired by the motive of avoiding trouble.

Because of the importance of inside-outside relationships for the under-standing of Thai social life, it makes sense to elaborate their classification somewhat more. One's relationships with the outside are pragmatically motivated by a desire for gain *(phonprayot)*, and are therefore superficial when compared with the deeper relationships with near persons. Toward distant persons one shows external presentation and invests honour and prestige; among intimates one shows genuine responsibility and invests friendship and kindness. In the outside world one needs to care for oneself and fight one's own battles, but the smaller world of trusted intimates cares for its members and functions as a centre of stability in spite of its lack of power. One needs to participate in the world outside, but one does not feel obliged; towards one's inside world one is committed.

The essential characteristic of unequal moral, or inside relationships is therefore trustful solidarity. As soon as one encounters the outside, its hierarchy is felt to be oppressive because of overwhelming power and basic unreliability. Toward the inside one feels *krengchai*, toward the outside *kreng-klua*. The inside is known for its goodness and reliability, and we could call this interaction with near persons interaction in the *khuna* dimension; behaviour in the outside could then be called interaction with power, or interaction in the *decha* dimension.

This is not to say that hierarchy is invariably seen as something negative. Many bosses create *bunkhun* relationships with their personnel, and persons may eagerly look for such beneficent sources of dependence. Such protectors serve as refuges *(thiphung)*, and their patronage is also called *bunkhun*—but with a difference. The *bunkhun* that one receives from a patron does impose a moral obligation that is contractual and temporary; one has to ask for it and then reciprocate, very much along the line of 'to ask and vow, and to then redeem the vow' *(bon kae-bon)*.

The complexities of the *bunkhun* concept in Thai social relations were recognized by Titaya Suvanajata (1976) when he observed that *bunkhun*-inspired closed personal relationships are the key to the stability of Thai social life, while formal relationships are inspired by pragmatic motives and not entertained for their own sake. The mixing of distant and intimate interactions occurs when *bunkhun*, or at least some sort of moral obligation, enters into relationships of unequal power, such as in the widespread phenomenon of patronage. The deepest, or most moral, *bunkhun* occurs in the closed personal relationship with one's mother, and that should be the most stable of Thai social relationships. The further one moves away from home, and the more hierarchical power enters the relationship, the greater the tendency toward instability, pragmatic motivation, and potential shifts in allegiance and loyalties: such relationships can be broken off in good conscience.

Independence and identity

As long as one is within one's trusted groups and immersed in moral *bunkhun* relationships, one should be loyal, reliable, trustworthy and trustful, and one should perform according to one's position among one's extended and classificatory kin. One feels at home, relatively intimate, and mutually dependent; these feelings are naturally accompanied by responsibilities. As a part of the group one is identified with it. The group is conservative and follows its norms and traditions and, although it will be tolerant and even defend its members, they should be careful not to provoke loss of its reputation by silly or irresponsible behaviour towards or in the presence of outsiders.

The solidarity of near persons serves as a refuge that is felt to be sure, inalienable and permanent; because of this safety-net function, a person may allow himself some personal independence that may be expressed in economic risk-taking, including borrowing money and gambling, in finding new solutions for one's own or communal problems, in migration, and even in such independence postures as expressing strong personal opinions or exhibiting a certain male irresponsibility, all of which are to an extent expected and sometimes admired. The young men especially are allowed a tolerated rowdy phase, for which working in town seems to be a kind of functional equivalent for girls.

Thai communities, in spite of their conservatism and tendency to social conformity, often lack adequate mechanisms to enforce moral behaviour, which in its turn allows for some individual deviation. The absence of strong mechanisms of social control, such as physical compulsion and violence, is compensated for by self-policing moral dependence as embodied in *bunkhun* relationships. To maintain one's self-respect and to avoid ostracism, the total complex of one's felt dependence on one's primary group ultimately functions adequately to keep most people in line. The good person remains dependent on the judgements of his near others and fears to 'sell face', this bringing shame on himself, or worse, on his group.

The stability of the group is promoted by a vague but omnipresent fear of rejection, often expressed in the threat to young children of 'being given away' (no rare occurrence, including 'being given away' to the monkhood or to foster parents, or even, for girls of poor families, being sold). To suffer rejection means that one has to operate in a dreaded, unreliable external world and to live by oneself. The desire for positive acceptance and identity within a trusted small world is therefore enhanced by the spectre of loneliness or the fear of being exposed to relationships that cannot be trusted. Such mechanisms are generally sufficient to keep persons in line while allowing them a certain degree of personality expression.

Typology and continuum

In the above we distinguished between interaction in the *khuna* and the *decha* dimension. The first type of association is characterized by familial hierarchy, moral *bunkhun* relationships, the *krengchai* attitude, and features trust and solidarity; because of these qualities, *khuna* relationships would seem basic to one's personality formation, self-respect, and definition of identity.

The *decha* dimension is characterized by powerful hierarchy, pragmatic *bunkhun* relationships, the *krengklua* attitude, featuring suspicion and uncertainty; because of these latter, such relationships are superficial and not deeply involving; they are instrumental for protection and material security.

When we envision a continuum between these *khuna* and *decha* poles, we can classify most regular behaviour. The stability and predictability of interactions would appear to depend upon the quality and the amount of the *bunkhun* involved. The relationships with near others on the familiar *khuna* side would be deeply obliging and extend over time, while the *bunkhun* generated by a good patron would be more pragmatic and only temporarily obliging. Further to the *decha* pole, the time frame of relationships shrinks, purposes becoming increasingly opportunistic and/or businesslike, until the moral content inverts, such as in extortion and theft.

Apart from the more purely commercial transactions, relationships always have a hierarchical—and thus moral—content that even surfaces in dyadic, that is, paired exchange relationships, such as the exchange of labour for productive or ritual purposes, in which the burden of indebtedness oscillates. This obliging quality of most interpersonal relationships also gives them a psychological content that is felt as a greater or lesser degree of emotional restraint.

Counterpoint behaviour: relaxed interaction

The above continuum allows for the classification of morally loaded, oppressive, and impersonal businesslike relationships but excludes the relaxed bonds between friends and peers where reciprocity is equally divided, where one does not expect *bunkhun*, and where *krengchai* simply means courtesy and not an intrinsic burden on the relationship. Informality *(khwam pen kan-eng)* is perhaps the best word to describe these relationships that are free and without inhibition, and therefore direct and relaxed. Without inhibition, though, is an overstatement. Virtually all Thai relationships are characterized by a measure of reserve, and yet, paradoxically, the Thais are masters of relaxation, an area where westerners, in spite of, or perhaps because of their 'confrontational intimacy', often fail. My best Thai friend may lend me money and only let me know through an intermediary when he needs that money again, without ever telling or showing me directly. This example shows the limits of Thai intimacy and the gentleness that guides it. People do not reproach a friend for having gotten drunk; while he was drunk, they coped with the situation. Nor does one expose all personal problems and frustrations, and deeper feelings are to be kept to oneself; they should remain unvoiced and are most often not even raised to the level of consciousness.

Yet, as observed earlier, the Thais are masters of relaxation, and are most relaxed and uninhibited in the company of peers and good friends, with whom they are not necessarily very intimate. This is the reality of *khwam pen kan-eng*, of mutual informality. In such situations, people do not need to maintain the façade of presentation, but speak their mind (though not their psyche), and enjoy the pleasure of direct access, being inquisitive, hospitable, boastful, generous, tolerant, unobliged, relaxed, and often bawdy among the members of the same sex. It is the occasion to sublimate frustrations and to relax.

It is in this kind of association that we find the behavioural counterpoint to hierarchical and unequal interaction. It is a much sought after situation where one feels amused and enjoys an atmosphere of pleasantness: it is *sanuk* in a profound sense of the word. One need not be shy, nor to be committed or easily embarrassed, because there is no need to either fear power or to bear the obligations of *bunkhun*.

This casual behaviour with non-intimate familiars is more relaxed than trustful and does not allow the individual to fully express himself. Thai culture does not prepare for personal openness, but rather warns against making oneself vulnerable or weak by exposing one's deeper emotions. Consequently, relaxed interaction remains on the surface and offers no psychological depth. It is therefore small wonder that it is often established with non-classified outsiders and may even bridge unusually large age gaps while still resulting in a comfortable atmosphere.

The individual reaction

Privacy and individualism are often used western concepts—even values— that are hardly applicable to any Thai reality. Thai life is public, or rather, is played out in public. This is not to say that the Thais do not recognize the existence of the individual personality; they do, and most people are further familiar with the Buddhist wisdom that a man ultimately depends upon himself and therefore needs to be self-reliant *(ton pen thiphung khong ton).* Yet, how to develop this quality remains vague; it is a search that one must experience and explore by oneself, and about which there is little culturally recommended content. Some people may meditate, others may indulge in daydreams and float in their fantasies, others again are tortured by frustrations and feelings that they keep to themselves; some get ill because of pressures and try not to show it; not a few men resort to boastful machismo behaviour; quite a few try to go it alone. But basically private affairs should be kept private, and to this type of privacy a Thai has both a right and an obligation. He must solve—or at least hide—his own psychological problems, and most people seem to be able to do this within the context of expected behaviour and its relaxed counterpoint.

A large segment of reality experience remains hidden within the personality, and that segment—from a cultural perspective—just belongs there and is entirely one's own affair. Such secret feelings and personal problems are mysterious and fearsome, and should be excluded from relationships that are guided by self-restraint and inhibition; yet sometimes suppressed emotions erupt as illness, stress, drunkenness, suicide or revenge.

A part of the personal experience can obviously not be expressed in a socially acceptable way and must therefore be suppressed. The person who is his own master, who plays it cool and does not allow himself to be greatly disturbed by the pressures of life, has found the ideal way to a measure of positive independence. If he shows his opinions and convictions he may endanger himself socially, but as long as he goes his own way without disturbing others, especially superiors, he will be accepted and privately admired. One definitely has a right to oneself and the society does not have a full claim on its members.

The self-reliant person is not easily upset by adverse social judgement or adversity; he is a master of the art of re-establishing equilibrium after unpleasant experience and cultivates a cool heart *(chaiyen)* so as to live undisturbed and sure of himself. He has an actively engaged attitude with a self-reliant personality in the centre and is able to solve his own problems. His *mai-pen-rai* ('never mind', 'you did not hurt me') is an expression of optimism, because he is involved without being attached. Consequently he may be sought out to become a refuge or leader of the many who are not so self-secure.

A more widespread response to cope with the pressures of hierarchical or obligation-inducing society is to cultivate the *choei* attitude as a kind of self-reliance. This attitude is a passive response, best translated as 'indifference', a temporary denial of and emotional non-participation in immediate reality, which is positively valued. Do not let the self be affected, cultivate detachment and resignation, because there is little or nothing that one can do to manipulate circumstances. It is the attitude of 'let it be', to which one has a right—that is, the right of not being bothered or disturbed. In this case *mai-pen-rai* translates as 'It doesn't matter' or 'I am not involved.'

Summary

The three positive responses to the constraints inherent in most behaviour on the *khuna-decha* continuum are the quest for relaxation in pleasurable, *sanuk* interaction, and the *chaiyen* and *choei* attitudes. They are probably also the very expressions of behaviour that give Thailand the reputation of being The Land of Smiles, peopled by a kind of mythological inividualists. That individualism—replete with its loose-structure connotations—can now be understood in the light of the rules of *decha* interaction, where opportunism and pragmatism logically prevail.

Closest to the western concept of individualism is the self-reliant *chaiyen* attitude; such self-reliance does not necessarily imply being socially responsible, though such responsibility definitely belongs to respectable western individualism. The Thai attitudes do not really correspond to notions of individualism or privacy, that are thus better left out of any discussion of Thai behaviour. Generally speaking, Thai relationships, and the attitudes and values that guide and inform them, are so culture-specific as to warrant distinctly Thai concepts—and terminology—as tools for analysis. It is only in terms of such categories that we shall be able to write a Thai theory of action.

Thai interaction can, however, be classified according to its *khuna* and *decha* elements along a continuum that corresponds to basic classifications. The family, with the mother at its centre, provides the moral model for all relationships (see next chapter). As the moral paradigm par excellence, it is applied to more distant, hierarchical, yet still personal, relationships with patrons and *phuyai* in the world outside. When relationships become less personal, while shading off into anonymity, they will be increasingly less obliging, more businesslike, and gradually dominated by the perceptions of amoral power, as exemplified in political practice. There the grasping of power serves the private interests of political bosses and their factions, and the use of power seems to have little to do with considerations of the common good, public welfare, or national solidarity (chapter 10).

HOLY MOTHER, MOTHER DEAR . . . HOW TO BE A THAI MOTHER

Thailand, the Land of Smiles, is known for the charm of its women and is also thought to be a bachelor's holiday paradise. It is known for serene Buddhist temples and also for Thai boxing, probably the toughest form of pugilism. As is often said, the Thai have a smile for every emotion, and whereas the gracious smile of one woman may underline her unassailability, it may be another woman's invitation. The peaceful temple preserves the Buddhist Path, and may also serve as a training ground for kick-boxing.

All these contrasts can be understood by reflecting on the remarkable separation of the male and female domains in life. The Thais like women to be beautiful and charming, virtuous and unassailable. Yet, simultaneously, the men also seem to have a strong need for other women to express their virility. They also box. And become monks.

While women seem to represent beauty and virtue—the two elements are almost fused in Thai thinking—men are supposed to be able to dominate the wider world and express their manliness in the brothel and the ring, in politics and religion. In that last area, women need them most.

As monks, men are representatives of the virtue of Buddhism, and of the sacred and its power. Monks provide a fertile field *(nabun)* that enables people to cultivate the merit they need to enhance their chances for a better rebirth, or even for the improvement of their current circumstances. Though gaining merit is not an exclusively female preoccupation, women are thought to gain tremendous merit by having a son ordained in the temple.

But why should a young man bother to engage in the disciplined life of a monk when there is so much more fun and excitement in the world outside?

Of course, there may be many reasons, such as poverty or the quest for an education, but the traditional motivation will also hold for most, namely, to make merit for one's parents, especially for mother.

In Thai education, the idea is inculcated that mother is the most important of persons. She has given life to the child, suffering for and feeding it at great psychological and physical cost to herself. What's more, she is the source of love and care, and she gives all freely. This tide of goodness results in a moral debt on the side of her child, a debt that it is never able to repay.

The only thing that the child can do to reciprocate is to love its mother. This love is expressed in being obedient to her, in considering and anticipating her feelings, and in showing gratitude and respect. Not to do so would imply the denial of the goodness of the mother, a repudiation that would come closest to the western notion of sin—also because such behaviour is believed to invite immediate supernatural retribution. No wonder that mother succeeds in imprinting herself very deeply on the emotional life of her offspring. Which is why making the sacrifice of becoming a temporary monk is an expression of filial devotion.

As a source of goodness, mother symbolizes virtue and selflessness. She is the pivot of one's moral obligations that revolve around the family. Her purity symbolizes the wholeness of the home. It is thus not too far-fetched to conclude that mother easily becomes the foremost reference point of one's conscience, that conscience is consciousness of her, and that she is the primary superego representative of most Thais.

This way of thinking may shed light on a curious phenomenon, the vast production of mother-centred literature. When I first ran across the collection *Mother Dear*, I was truly amazed at finding some sixty short stories and poems devoted to Mother, written by all kinds of notables, such as army officers, medical doctors, government ministers, well-known nobility, and so on and so forth. Soon I found out that almost all Thai authors write one or more short stories, and sometimes whole novels, about mothers, presumably their own.

Needless to say, this literature is really boring. Apart from eulogizing Mother, it invariably depicts her in the terms the Thai ideology requires. She is not a person any longer, but the symbol of virtue and sacrifice, of goodness and forgiveness. Yet, also in the general literature, it is very difficult indeed to find flawed mothers, mothers of flesh and blood who act as normal living people.

Thus I was very happy the day somebody told me about a collection of short stories written by a practising female psychiatrist.[1] Five of the six stories are about the mother-child relationship, and indeed, the author tries to bring more life to the character of the mother, some of whom she describes as cruel, non-caring and non-protective. But even she does not dare to go clear against the grain; on the contrary, toward the end of her stories it is the children who recognize that their mothers are the best of persons, and that it was their own perceptions which were at fault.

Obviously, the mother image is inviolably sacred. Having been virtually canonized, the ideological fog surrounding her position seems to be particularly dense. By becoming the symbol of Thai morality, she is placed beyond the ordinary world of men and everyday life. There she presides alone, she is the Holy Mother on earth, where Catholics have the Holy Virgin, or the Chinese their Kuan Yin.

Ideologically, mother stands on the lonely pedestal that seems to be her place in many societies that cultivate a virility complex, whether it is Mexican machismo or Latin he-manship. In that nexus, it is men who compulsively strive to steal the show, not so much to outdo women, but in competition among themselves. They like to indulge in boastful behaviour, demonstrating their masculinity by drinking and fooling around with women. They relegate their wives to the home, where she should fulfil the role of moral mother, who is not supposed to be a lover. The area of erotic adventure is completely outside the home, where one finds a different type of woman.

It appears that roles are firmly prescribed and that people find their security in conforming to role expectations. For the Thai husband, these expectations focus on his duty to provide for his family, while the other expectations about his virility should be proven in the world outside. And whereas Thai women occupy all kinds of positions in public life, they are supposed to find their fulfilment in the roles of mother and wife. In these positions, they should defer to men and accept the latters' privileged status. Inevitably, this separation of domains keeps men and women at a distance from each other, a distance that marriage most often maintains or even reinforces rather than bridges.

In Thailand, the competition for status and power appears to be intense, often giving rise to a lively political spectacle. Beyond the smile and female gracefulness, one finds the authoritarian ethos of a highly hierarchical society characterized by the struggle for power and personal prestige. It is conflicts of interest, and the fact that face can so easily be lost, that make the country a rather violent place, with an unusually high murder rate.

So, in parallel with the serene Buddhist temples and the mother-centred home, one finds the male area of contention and strife, that contrasts with the dependable area of existence that is symbolized by things female. The good things in life, such as the earth on which we depend for a living, the rice that nourishes us, the water that sustains life, and the guardian angel that protects the young child—all of them are represented as female, such as Mother Earth, Mother Rice, and Mother Water, among others.

It is not really in question whether an ordinary Thai woman can even begin to aspire to live up to the image of goodness and morality that the Thai ideology assigns to her. In daily reality, she is firmly of the world, and in the mundane realm she should above all be reliable. This is the role that Thai culture assigns to her: to be dependable as a wife and a mother, to be the stable point in a world that allows males to gamble and gallivant, to seek adventure and self-aggrandizement.

The male world means risk, politics and prestige. Men are consequently vulnerable, easily offended, liable to loss of face in their quest for glory. Basically, theirs is a competitive world, and where the risk of disappointment is so high, they need the compensation of a stable home to relax in, and to nurse the injuries to their self-esteem that they suffer in the world outside. Emotionally, they therefore lean far more on their mothers and wives than the latter do on them. In a way, many men remain boys, a kind of grown-up son (lukchai khon to) to their spouses.

In practice, the woman is thus one-up on the man, and this substantiates her title to him, gives reason for her possessiveness. By serving others, the woman stakes out her claim to be their conscience, so, in effect, it is her reliability that constitutes her bargaining power vis-à-vis her male, who depends on her psychologically to provide the secure base for his forays into the external world. As the Thai say, she functions as 'the hindlegs of the elephant', through her strength sustaining the great show of masculinity that would crumble without her support.

Most Thai women are quite pragmatic about all this. Where many men often appear to be wishy-washy, spoiled, cocky, and carried away by the greatness of their schemes, the women are generally hard-working, responsible and conscientious. They can, and do, take a lot. In spite of this, they normally maintain their good humour and their grace, contributing to the mystique of Thailand as The Land of Smiles. Let nobody be mistaken, though. In the male dominated world of Thailand, a smile may mean anything, from defence to submission, from politeness to subservience, and behind smiling female grace and elegance, one often finds powerful, go-getting women. Nevertheless, even given all that, the Thais appreciate grace and elegance; things should be beautiful to be in order, yet this order also requires hard work and dependability. Which is why it is women who are at the heart of Thai life.

INDIVIDUAL AND SOCIETY
IN MODERN FICTION

After the end of the Second World War, several Thai authors began to write socially critical novels which were intrinsically modern in the sense that they strove to raise the awareness of their readers about the structural and cultural conditions of Thai social life. In their elaboration and search for solutions, however, such novels are clearly the heirs to an older moralistic tradition of Thai writing, which emphasized right moral behaviour and wise personal ethics as the foundations of a good society. From the tension between the modern and the moralistic approach arose the idealistic progressive novel. The two outstanding representatives of this genre are Seni Saowaphong (the pen name of Sakchai Bamrungphong, a retired diplomat) and Siburapha (the pen name of Kulap Saipradit who died in exile in Peking in 1974).

These two authors were preoccupied with intellectual and moral emancipation. They strongly believed in the possibility of a better future that would bring freedom from oppression, so long as people grew conscious of their circumstances and became motivated by humanitarian ideals. It is no wonder, then, that they were taken as heroes by the student generation that overthrew the Thanom-Praphat dictatorship in the October uprising of 1973. For the students, the idealism of these authors provided a guide for their own desire to establish a better, more equitable society.

Both authors produced precursory novels set in a foreign environment before moving on to tackle the problems of inducing change and modernization in Thai society. Seni Saowaphong's first humanitarian novel, *The Love of Wanlaya (Khwam rak khong Wanlaya,* 1952), was set in Paris, with a cast of Thais and other people of diverse social backgrounds and preoccupations. Wanlaya, a female student of lower middle-class origin, is the pivot around whom these characters circulate, while discussing their views of life. She is the progressive figure who holds the view that it is not enough merely to live and struggle to establish one's own position, but that one should devote oneself to building a positive future for one's fellow men. Wanlaya's 'love', as used in the title, is love for humanity and its struggles. Her selfless passion is contrasted with motives of egoism and egotism, exemplified by the career motivations of a young Thai diplomat who sacrifices his wife and child to his ambitions. Social consciousness is illustrated in the story of a young Thai seaman who, through his contact with a Spanish labourer, is made aware of class solidarity, and the bright future that awaits proletarians of all countries if they unite. Seni further raised the question of the social relevance of art in the person of a lonely surrealist painter. When confronted with the ideas of Wanlaya, he switches his allegiance over to the social realist school, a shift which subsequently brings him friends and companionship.

The Love of Wanlaya is at best a theoretical treatise on idealism. It elucidates the social consciousness and personal ideals of the author, and it is therefore very comparable to Siburapha's *Until We Meet Again* (*Chonkwa rao cha phop kan ik*, 1950). This latter novel is set in Australia, where a privileged Thai student gradually develops a sense of social responsibility through his encounter with two young women who question the world in terms of justice, and demonstrate a dedication to humanity in their work.

Both Seni and Sriburapha subsequently dealt with their pre-occupations in a Thai setting. It is in *Evil Spirit* (*Phisat*, 1953) and *Look Forward* (*Lae pai khang na*, 1955, 1957), respectively, that they unfold their visions of Thai society and the ways in which it should develop into a better one. The fascination of both novels is that the authors tried to develop a full picture of Thai society, and the perceptions and ideas that inform it. In the power of their social imagination, both books were ahead of their times, and these pioneering 'modern' novels are still relevant to a contemporary under-standing of the development of Thai society.

In *Evil Spirit*, Seni introduces Sai Sima, who is the son of a poor peasant family. Due to his intelligence, and through the patronage of a monk, he finally becomes a lawyer. In spite of conflicts of loyalty, he consistently sides with the plight of the poor and exploited villagers of his background, and devotes himself to the task of making Thailand a just society. His relationship with a high-class girl makes her aware of the conceited view of the life of her peers. Sai thus becomes the embodiment of the 'evil spirit' of change, responsible for the awakening of the common people that threatens the position of the entrenched and privileged ruling class.

Evil Spirit opens perspectives into Thai life as seen from the positions of both the underdog peasants and the self-indulgent yet stagnating ruling class. The main characters are a group of university students of divergent backgrounds and ethnic origins (Thai and Chinese) who come to know each other during the course of their rejection of the dominant Thai values of hierarchy and willing submission. The development of the novel clearly implies a protest against the Thai social order, yet no programme for political action emerges. Society is clearly unjust, but injustice and the arrogance of the elite are seen as being fought by the personal example of lone idealists. Consequently, all the main characters act out their idealism by devoting themselves to the betterment and enlightenment of the poor and deprived people of Thailand.

Though Siburapha's *Look Forward* is very similar to Seni's novel, his characters are set in a more precisely defined historical period, from the absolute monarchy through its overthrow, and then on into the period of fledgling democratic ideals up to the early years of the Phibun Songkhram dictatorship. *Look Forward* is a novel in two parts, the second being left unfinished. In the first volume, *Youth* (*Pathoma-wai*, 1955), we witness the vicissitudes and good fortune of Chantha. The son of poor and suffering peasants, he arrives in Bangkok to further his studies, supported by the sponsorship of a monk. Subsequently, he is enabled to study at high school through the patronage of a ranking aristocrat, in whose compound he comes to live as a kind of a privileged servant. Later, he becomes an official in a ministry as a result of the same high backing.

Chantha's life story enables the author to provide glimpses into the life of peasants, and their exploitation at the hands of both officials and gangsters, into their suffering from natural events and bad health, and into the poverty and the exacting but upright life in a temple in Bangkok. Through such techniques as the portrayal of status competition among the retainers clustered together in the compound of the aristocratic patron, by his depiction of the interaction between teachers and pupils of the most diverse origins at an elite school in the capital, and in his elaboration of all kinds of situations that cut across class lines, the author gradually fleshes out a full picture of Thai society.

The second volume of the novel, *Middle Age* (*Matchimma-wai*, 1957), has a more explicit political content, which describes the deceptive evolution of Thai political life after the 1932 'revolution'. As in the first book, the development of the protagonist, Chantha, remains vague, the turbulent ambience of the changing times being personified and acted out by the secondary characters that surround him, such as former classmates, fellow students at Thammasat University, teachers, and other associates. This strategy suffices for the author to develop an elaborate panorama of the ideas and thought patterns of the progressive and democratic generation of that period. These enlightened ideas contrast with the reactions of the aristocratic class, and the ascendent military, who were to become the decisive new factor in Thai political life. Towards the novel's end, Chantha has become an up-country assistant prosecutor, in the hope of serving the peasant class from which he came in its quest for justice.

Sriburapha was a utopian socialist who believed in the possibility of the emancipation of the people. If—he speculated—everybody could enjoy equal opportunity, especially in education, while simultaneously developing a sound political consciousness, then all social problems would necessarily evaporate, and the end result would be an ideal society. This was why he lamented a hierarchical society's suppression of personality development and individual consciousness. In his view, structural barriers between the classes prevented communication, suppressing the lower class while isolating the upper class, and leaving both guided by 'false consciousness'. Confined by their limited social experience, people appear to be doomed to self-centredness and narrow-mindedness, which in their turn are the main causes for the lack of social justice.[1]

Both Seni and Siburapha were moralizing authors who presented their pictures of society in strong stereotypes, with their characters representing ideas, rather than flesh-and-blood people who come to life on the page through embodying psychological motivation. Individual experience is explained by social setting, and by the formula perceptions and expectations that belong to it. Twenty years later, we still find these qualities in the autobiographical works of another major novelist, Bunchok Chiamwiriya (the pen name of Nat Suphalaksuksakon, born in 1933).

Bunchok is a prolific author who writes about circumstances with which

0he is intimately familiar. Highly educated, with a master's degree earned in the United States, he became a District Officer. If it had not been for his remarkable personality, inspired by honest idealism and compassion for the people he had to administer, his potent talent as a writer would perhaps never have emerged. He became disaffected, however, with the corrupt and exploitative practices of government and, fired by his indignation, he left the civil service in disgust to go his own way.

His first and, to date, most successful novel, *The Revolutionary District Officer* (*Nai amphoe patiwat*, 1975), relates the experiences of a District Officer, and the moral dilemmas inherent in that position. Written in an ironical tone, the book delineates the tension between integrity and power, contrasting respect for human dignity with sycophancy and career motivations, fair administration with exploitation of the poor, and similar dichotomies. The book's focus is the life and practice of the provincial civil service and its relationships with influential Chinese merchants and the powers-that-be in Bangkok. Because the District Officer's moral integrity is at odds with the greed and self-interest of the civil service, the protagonist cannot be kept in his position. He is deemed 'revolutionary' because he is honest and committed to the welfare of the people that he has come to serve. These themes are further elaborated in *Black Sky* (*Fa sidam*, 1977), a subsequent attempt to explain the moral choices of the 'revolutionary' District Officer. Both of these works seem to have struck a chord with Thai readers, and have become unprecedented best-sellers.

Bunchok's most penetrating novel is his voluminous *The Human Element* (*That manut*, 1978). Its themes are the same, namely the injustice and exploitation perpetrated on people who are just, sincere, and earnest in a society where amoral and immoral power reigns supreme; where 'justice' can be bought, the honest suffer from oppression, and hypocrisy leads to reward. The setting is a vast urban society, Bangkok, and the world of unscrupulous publishers and impoverished struggling authors, the pirating of copyright, and the vagaries of the justice system. Altogether, *The Human Element* constitutes a powerful indictment of urban Thai society, with its selfish mentality and overwhelming indifference to the plight of the powerless.

In his latest writing, Bunchok describes his youth in the trilogy comprised of *Born in the Countryside* (*Koet ban-suan*, 1979), *To Be Born Means to Fight*

(*Koet laew tong su*, 1980), and *The Young Student* (*Nisit num*, 1981). In some passages, this series of novels exhibits remarkable similarity with Siburapha's *Look Forward*; the main character, Kla, however, is more independent and learns more quickly from life's experiences than his counterpart Chantha. Yet both are products of the poor countryside and both find patronage to further their studies, and it is through their confrontations with a great variety of people and situations that the authors succeed in evoking a picture of Thai social life in all its diversity.

These three novelists provide a critical yet somewhat stereotyped analysis of life in modern Thai society. Their novels belong to an older moralizing tradition, in which characters embody qualities and traits rather than becoming convincing living personalities. While such abstractions may be a concession to Thai taste and perceptions, it often makes for tedious reading when compared with the more penetrating and immediate descriptions of life by the extremely gifted short story writer Lao Khamhom (the pen name of Khamsing Srinawk, born in 1930 and now working in Nakhon Ratchasima province).

Khamsing is of Northeastern peasant origin and also writes about the underdog in Thai society, especially about their limited aspirations and the bitter fruits of their striving, their naivety and suffering, plus the reasoning and personal motivations that characterize life in the countryside. The strength of his stories derives especially from wonderfully evoked empathy and from exceedingly keen observation. His compelling interpretations and implicit social criticism are clear, yet he leaves it entirely to the reader to draw his own conclusions.

Khamsing expresses his commitment in the titles of his collections. The first, *No Barriers* (*Fa bo kan*, 1958; latest and enlarged edition 1979), voices his conviction that the high and the mighty do not have the right to suppress the poor and downtrodden of Thai society. Yet suppression is exactly what happened to his stories; Marshal Sarit Thanarat showed his displeasure upon the publication of his first collection, which was consequently not reprinted for quite some time. His writings were also disapproved of by the Thanin government that came to power in the counterrevolution of 1976, when Khamsing felt it prudent to go into voluntary exile. The title of his second collection, *The Wall* (*Kamphaeng*, 1975), refers to the wall that separates the urban Thai from the rural Thai, the powerful from the powerless, the privileged from the exploited. A selection of these short stories has been translated into English as *The Politician and Other Thai Stories* (1973).

In his succinct, and sometimes very brief, stories Khamsing reveals his mastery by saying a great deal in a very few words. In an intricate and subtle style coloured by a touch of mocking humour, he bares the matter-of-fact atrocities and self-centred motivations that lurk beneath the ideally smooth surface of social life. This revelation of underlying motives, of the fundamental conditions of poverty and ignorance, of baseness and suffering, have not helped to make Khamsing's writings widely popular. For the urban, educated Thai reading public, Khamsing's depictions are just too powerful; his caustic style and perception expose realities which most readers would prefer to deny—or at least to avoid.[2]

Such fastidious readers find it easier to empathize with the society-confirming works of minor authors such as Nimit Phumthawon. Once an up-country headmaster, he is one of the most prominent popular writers. He obviously identifies himself with peasant life and the school situations he writes about. His stories consistently exploit the conventional cognitive classifications that underly the Thai 'social construction of reality'. Mothers are self-sacrificing and good, teachers are either generous and righteous or else they turn into irresponsible drunkards who cannot adjust to the hardships of country life, village leaders are firm and protective of their villagers and do not shy away from the use of the gun when danger threatens, and village abbots are moral and wise. A major theme of Nimit's is that the relative peace of village life is threatened by dangerous gangsters and other quasi-criminal and power-hungry outsiders. Such characterizations pervade his novels *The Fragrant Smell of Grass* (*Hom klin dok o*, 1975), and *Headman Pho Choenchai* (*Kamnan Pho Choenchai*, 1977). A very similar picture of life in the countryside, and more authentic for that matter, is drawn by Prajuab Thirabutana in her charming autobiographical recollections, *Little Things* (1973; in English).

In a similar vein, the awareness of the educated urban upper middle class comes to life in the novels of Duangchai (the pen name of Prathumphon Watcharasathian). An associate professor of political science at Chulalongkorn University, she explores female reactions to a male dominated society. Her mildly progressive novels capitalize on the typical perceptions that inform the life of her class, yet they are nonetheless worth reading for their useful insights into the dilemmas of modern Thai women, and the problems of family life. Her most perceptive novels are *Stagnant Time* (*Huang sutthai haeng kanwela*, 1975), and *The Light of the Candle* (*Thian song saeng*, 1977).

Modern Thailand, being a relatively open society, allows the publication of a vast quantity of socially critical fiction and non-fiction. Social commentators, former political prisoners, politicians, disaffected civil servants and monks are among those who publish their thoughts and memoirs. Especially since the student uprising of 1973, a spate of short story writing has erupted, which aims at telling the 'true' conditions of Thai society. While analytically useful, most of these stories have been written from a 'social realist' perspective that often makes them quite dull as literature. The first full length novel along these lines is Rom Ratiwan's *The Fighter from the Northeast* (*Tonthewada naksu chak thirapsung*, 1980). This novel contrasts with his earlier stories, *Pui nun and duangdao* (1965), which are far more convincing in their authentic depiction of the meaning and experience of life in the countryside.

Commentary

The social scientist may draw tentative conclusions about the indigenous perception of social life from all sorts of written sources. Modern Thai fiction is an especially valuable one because the authors seem to 'address' their society. Their characters are always socially defined in types and roles that leave little room for psychological development. In a sense, this confinement contradicts the interpretations of an earlier generation of anthropologists who were impressed by a measure of Thai individualism (Evers, 1969). In the writings of Thai authors, individuals are almost always placed in clear and recognizable social settings that define them. If we contrast this with the depiction of the self-centred individual prevalent in current Javanese-Indonesian literature (Mulder, 2000: ch. 5), we may suggest that Thai individuals are more inclined to define themselves in their social setting and to see themselves more in terms of their status positions than as independent personalities.

The strong tendency to perceive other persons in terms of social types results in the tendency to symbolize certain social positions. With the exception of one atypical character in Duangchai's *Thian song saeng*, mothers are invariably compassionate and benevolent, sacrificing and forgiving, personifying the perfection of moral goodness *(bunkhun)* vis-à-vis their dependents. Mothers are portrayed as the very embodiment of virtue, and many Thai authors devote whole stories and even novels to this quality of the mother, Po Inthrapalit's *Mother* (*Mae*, 1976) being an example.

Similarly, the character of 'teacher' embodies important values. Often the teacher appears to be the male equivalent of 'mother', but as a man he may function as a bridge between the homely world of trust and the vast and daunting world outside. Combining the roles of goodness and wisdom (both sources of *bunkhun*) with masculinity, teachers are often depicted as the white heroes who oppose a wicked world. Fighting evil single-handedly, such as in Khamman Khonkhai's *The Teachers of Mad Dog Swamp* (*Khru bannok*, 1978; English translation, 1982), they often perish in the end, strongly suggesting that righteousness cannot win against amoral power.

In the writings of Bunchok, Nimit, and Duangchai, an inner world of trust and goodness appears to be systematically opposed by an unreliable and threatening world of power. Authors such as Seni, Siburapha and Bunchok protest against it, while Khamsing and the early Rom seem simply to acknowledge its existence. In all cases, life is unstable and informed by the fear of uncertainty and unreliability. Thus it is wise to seek safety and security in the inner world of family, relatives and community, as described by Nimit and Duangchai. In the novels discussed, this dualism is elaborated as a question of moral choice. The reading public appears to appreciate this identification of personal conduct with ethical behaviour. The good person applies the ethics of the inner circle to each and all, the 'revolutionary' District Officer being the perfect example in his protest against double standards and moral particularism.

All the authors discussed emphasize individual-centred ethics. Even in the more 'sociological' approach of Siburapha, society is not pictured as an organic, interdependent whole that is amenable to social engineering. To Siburapha, individual moral development is the wellspring from which good order is to flow. If, he seems to say, everybody enjoys an equal chance to better himself, and if we learn to have compassion for our fellow man, a just society will inevitably result. In *Look Forward* it is precisely the status order of Thai society that is seen to be the root of all its ills. In this, characters are depicted as the occupants of status positions who look out for themselves and their own self-centred interests. Yet what might be a better society of thinking and enlightened people remains unclear and undescribed, because its impulses are identified in individual moral and ethical behaviour. Therefore society appears as an aggregate of individual statuses that relate to each other in pairs, and no consolidated view develops.

CHAPTER 7

AVOIDANCE AND INVOLVEMENT: SUMMARIZING IDEAS ABOUT INDIVIDUAL AND SOCIETY

Cosmological and religious perspectives

Several Buddhist teachings have deeply influenced the Thai concept-ualization of 'being human'. Two central concepts are those of reincarnation and Karma. Whereas the latter may be understood as the inevitable progressions of the infinite chains of cause and effect through which the vast machinery of cosmic justice proceeds, in everyday practice it is taken to mean the present circumstances of one's personal lot (karma) in life. This is believed to be largely predetermined by one's positive and negative actions in previous existences, though also to some extent by one's deeds in the present one. In sum, each individual's fate is the outcome of what he has done during the course of innumerable life-spans; and since no two people share the same moral history, nobody can be like anybody else. Everybody has to work out, and through, his own destiny. Liberation comes about through one's own efforts.

Since both positive and negative acts result in accordant effects, periods of good fortune may alternate with periods of adversity, a cycle which reinforces the personal understanding of existential uncertainty. Yet, since previously accumulated karma may have been 'worked out', and thus only partly conditions one's experiences in the present, many people are aware of the need to depend upon themselves in shaping their present and future.

This self-dependent view of the person and his experience corresponds with the relative absence of the idea that human life is the manifestation of a supreme order to which one must submit oneself. If there is any order at all, it is the order of contingency and personal action, that is best expressed in the credo that both meritorious and demeritorious deeds produce accordant consequences. Basically, cosmic law—that is, the Law of Karma centres on personal moral and ethical behaviour, which gives rise to an individual-centred view of the order of life.

This creed of moral independence is balanced by the fact that one is born of parents and is completely dependent on their goodness *(bunkhun)* while growing up. This virtue of the parents places the child under the lasting moral obligation to honour and be grateful to them. To fail to fulfil this basic obligation is to commit the sin of *nerakhun*, or to 'rebuff goodness received'. Such a rebuffal is believed to be an extremely demeritorious act that will result in the immediate experience of bad karma.

Moreover, from an animistic perspective, the person knows that beyond his own moral resources, he can depend on and seek the protection of *saksit* power, which can help him to achieve his aims and enjoy a safe existence. In order to mobilize such supernatural protection, a person should perform a ritual supplication to some spirit for it. While there is a measure of volition in seeking this protection, it also conveniently shifts the burden of self-reliance to dependence on what is more powerful than oneself. This oscillation between perspectives of dependence and independence pervades the relationship between the individual and society.

Social perspective

Thai society organizes itself in a hierarchical fashion in which people occupy differently ranked positions. Most relationships, therefore, are characterized by relative superiority versus inferiority. To the Thai child, the social world appears at first as an aggregate of benevolent superiors. The centre of this sphere is its mother, on whose benevolent and loving care it depends. This dependence on the mother is widely idealized in Thai culture, she being the reliable centre of intimacy, faith and certitude in a basically untrustworthy world.

Yet mother's love does not come free, and as the child is being made to feel that it fully depends on its mother's goodness, it is also taught to reciprocate by the show of obedience. All superiors seem to be entitled to a child's respect as a matter of course, and one of the first things it is taught is to show this respect and to present itself politely. Soon the tot learns that a measure of 'subduedness' and conformity leads to reward and acceptance, and that many people are highly sensitive to the respect owed to their person.

Beyond the circle of benevolent superiors and near others—such as relatives, community members, or classmates—one finds the distant others who represent an awe-inspiring world of hierarchy and unpredictable power. In dealing with such outsiders, it is wise to be respectful, and wary of their motives. In effect, the child has to absorb the lesson that people are to be classified in terms of rank and distance, and its behaviour should be appropriate when dealing with each of these different catagories.

For some people, the hierarchical perception of others tends to become highly stereotyped, automatically equating persons with their rank and status. In a way, this isolates people from each other, and even though the acknowledgement of superior rank does not necessarily imply the recognition of authority over one's person, inferiors will often feel inhibited and restricted in their self-expression when in the presence of such people. Thus many people appear to be keen to guard a measure of autonomy in their social affairs, not easily committing themselves to others, while at the same time pragmatically seeking to promote their own ends.

As popular wisdom has it, "It is best to know how to take care of your own affairs and to stay out of trouble"; the person who is able to do both validates his self-respect. While, of course, it is wise to cultivate good working relationships with one's fellows, it is also shrewd and politic to keep them at some distance. This tendency to stay clear of each other leads to a remarkable tolerance of deviation and a weak measure of social control, a lenience that may reflect respect for the independence and individuality of others. The prime source of interpersonal integration appears to be the recognition of mutual obligations; this principle of reciprocity ties people together in an extended system of personalized, dyadic relationships. Communal integration tends to remain weakly developed; if strong leadership is not forthcoming, members of communities will generally only cooperate on the occasion of religious festivals or ceremonies.

The primary direction of integration among people appears to be vertical. Vertical integration is especially apparent in the patrimonially structured national organizations, for example, the civil service and the brotherhood of Buddhist monks *(Sangha)*. Yet even in more horizontally structured situations, people tend to interrelate in terms of relative status, social distance and extent of obligation, these social coordinates not only defining the other person but also oneself. Many people tend therefore to identify with their position, and to derive a good deal of satisfaction from recognition of their status.

To protect or advance such recognition, one may need to regularly validate one's status by, for instance, throwing a lavish party, or financing conspicuous religious merit-making. Among Thai men, this quest for recognition is often expressed in typical acts of virile behaviour, such as impressing others by their boldness, womanizing, or big-spending. In identifying with their own vanity, they try to enhance their presentation and may consequently become very vulnerable to questions of 'face', and likely to become stubborn and seek revenge if slighted.

Avoidance and involvement

The 'ethos of relative independence' that was propounded above becomes more meaningful if it is contrasted with the predominantly vertical dimension of hierarchy, and the obligation to pay visible respect to superiors. This suppresses individualism but seems to separate people from each other: it may lead some to almost total identification with their status and the respect owed it, while in others it will stimulate the desire to keep one's distance from other people in order to ensure some room for personal manoeuvre. It also leads to a quest for friends with whom one can share one's frustrations and displeasure at a life in society that often forces one to pose as a mere inferior.

Respect of hierarchy, obligation, and deferential manners are among the first things a child learns as it grows out of infancy. Children soon learn to feel apprehensive about their behaviour in the presence of superiors, and to become sensitive to all forms of criticism. Anxiety about presentation is known as 'shyness' *(ai)*. Such diffidence is rated positively by elders, and may stimulate the development of the Thai equivalent of self-mastery. Subsequently, children will learn to keep their emotions to themselves, but also discover that they can get their own way by the show of respectful and obedient behaviour.

To be bashful and shy, or 'to have a thin face', is a positive quality in people who restrain themselves and thus avoid giving offence to others. It is considered important to train children in solicitude and circumspection in facing others, especially strangers and superiors. This attitude should later mature into the more refined one of *krengchai*, which reflects awareness and anticipation of the feelings of others. *Krengchai* behaviour manifests itself in kindness, self-restraint, tolerance, and the avoidance of interpersonal irritation. The initiation in this lies with the one practising *krengchai*; such a person is considerate of others and puts much thought and effort into maintaining a smooth social atmosphere.

The behaviour of some people seems to be the product of an excess of *krengchai* that seemingly causes extreme reluctance to draw attention to oneself by actions, resulting in giggling and inertia. Such shyness, inspired by incipient feelings of shame or fear, can hardly be considered as positive 'consideration of the feelings of others'. Similarly, while relating to one's superiors, an avoidance of initiative coupled with an extreme concern to please the boss may lead to acceptance—but smells of sycophancy rather than *krengchai*. Even though it is sometimes difficult to draw the line between these two attitudes, it remains true that the *krengchai* attitude encourages people in the avoidance of unpleasantness and interpersonal confrontation.

Because of the general vulnerability of 'face', being circumspect about the motives of others is wise, while unconsidered criticism is dangerous. It is better to let the other have his way if one wants to achieve a measure of personal security, and a self-effacing attitude is the safest one to adopt for the relative inferior. Moreover, violence is endemic in Thai society and it is folly to 'build oneself an enemy'. Everybody knows that all are extremely vulnerable to affronts against their 'face' and that revenge for a perceived insult, however unintended, may have extremely unpleasant consequences. Especially with distant others, it pays to be careful. In such cases it is not necessarily *krengchai*, but sometimes a feeling of fear *(krengklua)* that is inspired by the distant other, which motivates the desire for total avoidance.

Often, Thai people seem to be highly aware of living in a dangerous world where one is constantly uncertain about the motives of others. On the one hand, this awareness may be a cause for the idealization of the mother-child relationship that has become the symbol of the only trustworthy and reliable relationship in the world. On the other hand, it may inspire the belief in the wisdom of watching out for oneself while staying out of trouble. Consequently, it is wise to practise non-involvement in the affairs of others, to be tolerant, and to go one's own way if possible. In respect to one's wider social surroundings, one soon learns the wisdom of remaining indifferent *(choei)* and of restraining oneself emotionally, especially when one has no power or influence. Politics, administrative decisions, government programmes or developmental schedules are all basically the affairs of others that one accepts or suffers without involving oneself. Yet, closer to home and in one's direct relationships with others, one may often be more involved than one would like.

However astute holding oneself aloof from others' affairs to avoid trouble may be in theory, in practice it often boils down merely to the mastery of social form, and not to the total eradication of negative emotions. By staying out of others' way and by avoiding undue intimacy, one may try to avoid emotional involvement that might rupture the ideal, smooth surface of social life. To present oneself politely is a good strategy to control situations, and the clichéd Thai smile is one of its manifestations. Although smiling and politeness give interaction a pleasant façade, it is often a mere self-defensive manipulation of form that keeps people at a distance from each other.

The relative importance of maintaining distance leads to the presumption that many Thai individuals may suffer from the lack of possibilities their society offers for self-expression. They seem not only to avoid emotional confrontation with others, but often also appear to be incapable of confronting their own inner selves. If this is true, then one might guess that the Thai person is highly involved with his presentation, not only as a means of achieving acceptance and status, but even physically, as a body that needs to be presented in the best of order. Often, it appears that outward acceptance spells inner security, and that the distance between one's accepted presentation ('face') and one's emotional self is small; Suntaree Komin refers to this connection as a strong 'ego orientation' (1990:161-4).

For acceptance and the recognition of status, a person may be dependent on others whom he would emotionally prefer to avoid. In many instances, these others are also the source of material security, and may even be superiors who treat one in such a way that ill-feelings arise that must be suppressed. Between these polarities of involvement and avoidance, of dependence and independence, the individual can only hope that the received wisdom of avoiding overt conflict may contribute to feelings of personal peace and satisfaction, and that the quest for fun and pleasure *(sanuk)* will provide sufficient release from frustration.

The individual perspective

In private life, individuals will tend to identify with role more than with position. Of course, 'mother' is both a role and a very important status, but in everyday life she performs a role first of all. In public, or with increasing social distance, individuals represent their position, while role and role expectations become vaguer. In wider society, people will be known and addressed by the most conspicuous position they hold, such as professor or air vice-marshal, abbot or wife-of-the-boss (*khunnai*). They are socially defined.

Role and status offer different anchoring points for the individual. Role inheres a measure of continuity and stability, and its performance depends very much on the individual concerned. Status or position, however, places the person in the hands of others who need to recognize that status and lend it the prestige it deserves. Status must be lived up to in a competitive public world. Despite status volatility, identification with position in public life tends to be high, and much emotion becomes invested in its presentation. This tendency allows for understanding public life as a show, a real theatre of life in which people present themselves as positions on an ever-changing map drawn according to the contemporary hierarchy of power and prestige.

Individual positions define people in relation to each other, and give rise to certain, mutually unequal expectations that crystallize in rights and duties. The individual is good as long as he or she performs accordingly, giving the respect due and fulfilling his obligations to the other. The individual is, therefore, identified by paired personalized relationships. The moral way that belongs to it may be called the ethics of (social) place that bring individual action into focus. These highlight the immediate environment—and its pressure for conformity—at the expense of the wider surroundings. Still, that whole is thought to benefit, to be in good order if all perform according to role and status. In a way, this makes the individual important: the orderly condition of society depends on individual performance.

Behind the socially anchored identities of status role and, we naturally find the person as an individual character, as somebody out of the social context as it were. Whatever is behind the social presentation is secretive, both for the other and for the person concerned. Presentation masks the latent whirlpool of emotions and drives. These should be left alone and out of sight: they may be explosive, threatening, and no good can come from them. Such individual characteristics have no place on the social scene.

The necessity of modifying self-expression to fit in with social surroundings is not to everybody's liking, and many people show a sturdy tendency to seek another path and go their own way. They try to stand on their own feet, and seem indifferent to the socially inspired self-identity with which most people have to content themselves. Such nonconformists show a good deal of courage and initiative in living as 'outsiders' in society. What they seek is a position in which they can escape the pressure to live up to the requirements of the hierarchy.

To be able to maintain oneself outside the frame of social compulsion is at the same time odd and admired. In order to do it, the individual is advised to cultivate self-mastery, a measure of aloofness and indifference (*choei*), and a 'cool heart' (*chaiyen*). This means not to allow oneself to be carried away by emotions, to avoid conflict, and to maintain one's dignity by refusing to be ground down by the pressures of social life. It means mastery of a situation by cultivating a measured distance and reserve while going one's own way. It is noninvolvement and indifference to considerations of 'face'. It also leads to the satisfaction of solving problems independently.

This last perspective on the individual is at least as old as Theravada Buddhist ideas circulating in Thai society. According to certain social critics, this is the type of person the country needs if it is going to give positive shape to life in the modern urban mass society. In that living space, people are anonymous to each other, and thus equal. There they have to operate without the constaints of the hierarchically defined social coordinates. There they must be self-dependent, take their own decisions, and hopefully be self-respecting and responsible. After all, urban living individualizes. Consequently, these social critics may have a point.

BUDDHISM, NATIONAL IDENTITY AND MODERNITY

Rapid social change often stimulates a quest for a reaffirmation of identity that is anchored in history and tradition. Whereas the future is elusive, the past provides a firm basis for identity definition in facing modernity and change. In the beginning of this century, King Rama VI (reigned 1910–25) formulated the three pillars of Thai unity, continuity, and identity as Nation, Religion, and King—religion being for all practical purposes Buddhism. An analysis of this great national institution in its identity function is the subject of this chapter.

Monkhood and population

Buddhism is the majority religion of Thailand, and to most Thais to be a Thai is equated with being a Buddhist. Apart from the massive government bureaucracy, the Buddhist monkhood (Sangha) is numerically the largest of all Thai institutions, but while attitudes toward civil servants are often ambivalent, attitudes toward monks are almost always positive and trustful. The bureaucrats are seen to embody the power to rule and command, but the monks represent a way of life in which all Buddhist Thais share. Buddhism is therefore the greatest of Thai institutions, expressive of and perpetuating the Thai nation, its traditions, its ritual, and its identity.

According to the 1976 statistics of the Ministry of Education, 95.92 percent of the Thai population declared itself to be Buddhists and these believers supported 25,702 temples with 213,175 monks, 114,792 novices, and 10,529 nuns nationwide.[1] This makes for an average of five temples *(wat)* per district *(tambon)*, or one monk to every thirty-eight adult Buddhist males. Combining monks and novices, we find some 328,000 men in yellow robes, making Buddhism most visible and ubiquitous. While it is possible to travel for days in remote areas without seeing a representative of government, it would be strange indeed if a day passed without seeing a living manifestation of Buddhism.

Why are there so many monks *(phra)* and novices? And who are they? It is a well-known cultural ideal that every man should ordain as a monk, normally for one *phansa*, or Buddhist Lent of three months during the rainy season, as a kind of rite of passage between adolescence and marriage. When we consider the official estimate of 75,000 temporary monks who enter and leave the monkhood each year and project this number against the group of 350,000 Buddhist males who are twenty years old, we find that only one in five still follows the dictates of tradition. These men, whether twenty years of age or older (many are officials or soldiers, granted a special paid leave to temporarily ordain), subject themselves to the Buddhist discipline for monks and study some rudimentary aspects of Buddhism during the three months (or less) that they are in the temple. They are recognized to be temporarily there and they do not really mix with the regulars who spend a longer period in the temple.

The real hard core of monks, that is those who spend ten or more years in robes and who make religion at least part of their lifework, numbers slightly over 30,000. Most of them will attain administrative office, such as abbot, or become teachers of Pali, meditation, and other Buddhist subjects. About a third may act as preceptors and ordain new monks into the order.

Beyond the temporary and the senior monks, there are left some 225,000 monks and novices to be explained. Nearly all of them come from the poor to very poor segment of the rural population, and their entering the monkhood is often prompted by economic reasons. Most of them see the monkhood primarily as the only chance for further education and, especially when they are recently ordained, as a fulfilment of tradition and an expression of filial piety towards their parents who gain great merit by having a son in robes. When they have exhausted the educational possibilities that the monkhood offers, most of them will disrobe and continue their careers as laymen; yet it is also from their ranks that most lifetime monks will be recruited. Assuming that on the average this middle group ordains for a period of three to five years, it would appear that 33–44 percent of the adult male Buddhist population has monastic experience of one sort or another.

To have spent some time in the monkhood still carries prestige and reaffirms Thai traditions. Especially those who have spent more than average time in the robes will be well versed in Pali formulae and the details of ritual; after disrobing they may acquire prestigious positions, such as leader of the lay congregation or member of the temple committee.

The primary attraction for the impoverished country boys to join the Sangha is the opportunity to go beyond the four years of primary school that is the minimum educational requirement for admission. Although the secular educational system of the Thai government is now spread all over the countryside and has penetrated into most outlying areas, these schools are still unable to provide all school-age children with the legally required six years of study. Moreover, formal school education is relatively expensive for poor parents; by sending one of their sons to the *wat* as a novice, they follow a somewhat prestigious and certainly meritorious path. Their son, they know, will be fed and cared for, and offered a unique chance to better himself.

Part of the temple education consists of acquiring a knowledge of chants, preaching, and of general religious instruction. The newly ordained learn to behave like monks, so that the laymen who support them can gain merit. This means that they should, at least publicly, stick to the rules of their discipline *(Vinaya)*, know how to participate in ceremonies, and generally behave so as to coincide with their laymen's expectations.

The other part of their likely education consists of a combination of formal religious courses *(naktham)* combined with the regular curriculum of government schools; the student novices and monks have to sit for the regular government administered examinations. By going to important temples in provincial capitals they can study up to the third and highest *naktham* level and the final year of high school; in the provinces, they can also study for the teachers' training certificate. If they aspire to higher levels of religious and secular education, they must study Pali, that is, the sacred language of Therevada Buddhism, in combination with the fourth and fifth year highschool curriculum. If they are successful in both, they may be admitted to study at one of the two Buddhist Universities in Bangkok. Eventually they are even sent abroad, mostly to India, to seek master's and doctoral degrees. As in the past, it appears that one of the important functions of Thai Buddhism is to provide an avenue of education and mobility for underprivileged men.

The main impulse of Thai schooling is to accumulate conventional knowledge. Education within the monkhood does not necessarily create a religious personality or stimulate any deep insight into the truths of Buddhism. Buddhist personality development depends on the wise seniors who befriend and guide a young monk according to individual personality factors. One may meet *phra* who have a deep understanding of Buddhism in any village temple, at any level of the hierarchy, yet not too often among those who devote much of their time to formal religious and secular studies. The connection between religious development and curricular knowledge appears to be weak. Therefore it is small wonder that most of the highly educated young monks leave the order before they have made a meaningful contribution to its development: they have been prepared for a life that is more meaningful outside the confines of the temple than inside them.

The situation that the educational opportunities offered to monks rather lead to disrobing than to a strengthening of the Buddhist institution, often leads to criticism from the more privileged laity. While there is some substance in their criticism, they should also ask the question where a poor man should get his education from if not a member of the monkhood. Most of the highly placed monk-administrators are inclined to defend the present situation by maintaining that the monkhood contributes to the good of society—which is closely linked to the well-being of religion—by training young monks who will not only be educated but also moral men who will contribute to the spiritual and material development of society, whether in the monkhood or not.

What is the situation that a young monk will face when he graduates? He may have acquired a lot of formal knowledge about Buddhism and may or may not have ideas about its social role, but he has also acquired ordinary ideas and knowledge of great value in secular life. Most graduates want to be progressive and to share their knowledge and education. They may be devout, practising Buddhists. Yet how are they going to achieve their ambitions while in the temple?

The Thai monkhood is extremely liberal and tolerant until a certain limit when it becomes extremely hierarchical, highly stratified, and the opinion of the elders cannot easily be circumvented. While there are a few mildly progressive members in the highest governing bodies of the monkhood, and while progressiveness is not even uncommon among the staff of the Buddhist universities, the atmosphere of the hierarchy tends to be stultifying and formal. It can seem even nonreligious in the sense that it concentrates only on the performance of the correct ceremony at the correct time, and not on bringing life to the essence of the Buddha Dhamma in contemporary society. The respect for hierarchy and tradition that once characterized Thai society as a whole is still fully alive in the religious establishment, so much even that the monkhood may well be judged to be the most old-fashioned of all Thai institutions; it lacks leadership, vision, purpose and inspiration beyond the guardianship of ceremonies and tradition. In that atmosphere there is little room for young bright people who want to perform or to reform.

Thus the better educated monks often leave the order, not just because they have achieved their educational goals, but they also leave because they feel that they will never stand a chance to clean up the cobwebs of complacency and traditionalism that pervade the upper levels of the hierarchy. If monks aspire to more than rank and honour, and if they want to make Buddhist thought relevant to modern life, then they are in for a hard time with little chance for success. They will necessarily be frustrated and tend to opt for a secular career. That decision is not their fault, but one of the system in which they live and have to seek their satisfaction (Mulder, 1973:26–8).

The idea of reform and revitalization is contemporary and alive only among those modern Thais, whether layman or monks, who question the current state of Buddhist practice (see below, Modernity means criticism). The possibility of change may even motivate a small number of modern monk-administrators to remain in the order in the hope of effecting some reform from within, while some other long-term monks may go their own independent way in a few meditation and propagation centres.

Most long-standing monks, however, appear to find satisfaction in their way of life, because they fulfil the functions that the vast majority of the Thai populace expect from having religion and having monks. In terms of career, a long-time monk often enjoys considerable prestige and respect, and many climb in the ranks of honour and office. As an abbot he may play an influential role in his parish and be consulted about all kinds of affairs. In addition to prestige, his way of life is not necessarily uncomfortable, and his forsaking of many of the pleasures of the world also protects him from much of its suffering and sorrow. There may be much role satisfaction in fulfilling the expectations of the populace and in being the ritual focus of a community in search of protection, guidance, auspiciousness and blessing. Most often from a humble background, the role of an accomplished religionist and mediator with the sacred may hold many more positive attractions than the fear of society or sheer laziness that also keep some men in the yellow robes.

In former days, the functions of the monkhood were diverse and the parish temple was clearly the centre of its ritual and social life. For any degree of education, villagers were dependent on what the *wat* could offer. The temple was the intellectual centre of the community, the place where one went for all kinds of general advice, medical healing, astrological consultation, dealings with government, or spiritual and practical counsel in times of difficulty. With the expansion of government services in education, communications, health care, and so on, most of these functions have greatly diminished in importance, but the religious function remains. The temple still safeguards tradition and mediates between the laymen and their needs for safety, auspiciousness, blessing and protection.

For most Thais there is no need for institution-building beyond what already exists. Their religious mentality neither asks for more, nor for less, and monks respond to the demand for these services. They serve as a field where people can cultivate merit *(na bun)*, and thus assure themselves of auspiciousness and continuity in the present and beyond. Monks extend blessings to institutions, things, and people, and it is through supporting them that the layman gains merit and beneficial karma *(kam)*. By living according to their discipline, monks already assure their laymen of auspiciousness.

The dependence on monks is most clearly expressed in death ritual *(phithi awamongkhon)* where monks are essential to guide the deceased out of the realm of chaos and doom into a better rebirth while safeguarding the peace of the living. Monks also play a role in most other transitional life-cycle ritual, such as marriage ceremonies, the occupation of a new home, and very particularly in the ritual acquisition of maturity when young males traditionally join the order of Buddhist monks for a Lenten period.

Apart from such orthodox activities, many monks have a reputation for occult skills, such as making amulets or holy water, for inserting protective power into Buddha images, for astrological calculation, for tattooing and other practices that ward off evil. In the eyes of many people, and sometimes in spite of their own more purely Buddhist intentions, monks also function as the source of white magical power that ensures the continuity and favourable blessing of the community, whether as village or nation.

Monkhood and state

With the exception of the very highest levels, the administrative organization of the Buddhist order closely parallels the organization of the state bureaucracy; in its elaborate hierarchical structure of grades, ranks, and honorary titles the monkhood reflects the status orientation of Thai society. While in villages the behaviour of monks and the appointment of abbots is under the control of the local community, at the higher levels of state, administration and policy-making, the monkhood is under the control of the central government, and all the higher appointments need to be sanctioned by the king. In the same way people depend on the participation of monks for their important rituals, such as the inauguration of a business, a housewarming, or the anointing of a newly bought airplane, so also do all important state ceremonies require legitimation by the presence and blessing of monks. As a nation-wide institution the monkhood is expressive of a cultural and religious communality in which all Thais participate.

Throughout history, Thai governments have been aware of the important integrative function of Buddhism and have repeatedly made efforts to control the monks and their practices, and to bring their organization under the supervision of the state. With the establishment of a truly national hierarchy, the standardization of the curricula for monks, and the promulgation of various legal acts on the administration of the monkhood (the last in 1962), state influence on the hierarchy above the village level appears to be decisive. Whereas the monkhood at large and individual monks are supposed to forego a political role independent of the state, the religious hierarchy is used as an instrument of state, serving the interests of national integration and development (Charoenkiat, 1977; Skrobanek, 1976).

In the 1960s, the missionary Thamma-charik programme was developed to reach non-Thais and non-Buddhist hilltribe populations in order to draw them through Buddhisticization into the mainstream of Thai life. Another missionary programme, Thamma-thut was aimed at remote Thai populations to strengthen their allegiance to the polity and to fight communism through ideological means. Simultaneously, and often inspired by the same anti-communist motive, monks were trained for community-development activities and sent up-country to promote the welfare of the village population. These programmes have met with a modicum of success but have also exposed the danger of involving monks in the affairs of the state: by identifying monks with political goals and as instruments of state, the unifying element of national religious expression and communality was jeopardized (Keyes, 1971; Mulder, 1973).

The danger of this role conflict came saliently to the fore during the turbulent days of democracy between 1973–76, when some monks joined in peasant demonstrations to show their identification with the poorer segments of the population, while other influential monks, such as Kittiwuttho Bhikkhu contrarily defended the establishment and even went so far as to declare that in his view it was Buddhistically a relatively minor sin to kill a communist because that death served the higher purpose of national stability. Politicization and polarization reached their zenith when the former leader Marshal Thanom Kittikhachon returned from exile as a novice and was immediately ordained as a monk in one of the most prestigious temples of Bangkok.

The identification of some members of the Buddhist hierarchy with the political right and some others—mostly common monks—with the left is clearly dangerous to the integrative function of Buddhism as a shared institution. Although the overt political involvement of certain monks has since abated, the institution of Buddhism as an integrative national symbol is felt to have come under threat by the visibility and influence of the Santi Asoke sect and its independent brotherhood of monks. At the same time, the Thammakai offers non-orthodox alternatives to established Thai Buddhist practice. Whereas the latter sect continues to operate within the framework of the national Sangha, the self-determination of the Santi Asoke stirred sufficient controversy—also for political reasons (chapter 1)—and its monks were ordered to change their dress from the characteristic saffron robe to something else—or otherwise to be detained as imposters.

More damaging to the public image of the Sangha is the avid publicity of the scandals caused by certain individual monks, ranging from corruption to membership in criminal gangs, from fraud in order to receive royal decorations to outright sexual misdemeanour, fatherhood, and violence against the women involved. Of course, old-fashioned preoccupation with rank and status, politicization, new sects, and the current flurry of scandals (Mulder, 1997:185–188) do not undermine the demand for monks as mediators of blessing, sacred power and auspiciousness, but do tarnish the image of the institution that Thais would prefer to see as a prestigious symbol of their national identity.

Buddhist education: the formal presentation of Buddhism

What should be taught—and what should not be taught—about Buddhism is a national and political affair that emerged clearly during the reign of Marshal Sarit Thanarat (prime minister from 1957–63) when he opposed the teaching of the *santosa* doctrine as being non-productive and an impediment to national development. The *santosa* doctrine teaches that one should find contentment and satisfaction in what one has, leading to a quiet, non-attached state of mind *(sunyata)*. In subsequent and widely publicized discussions between Buddhadasa Bhikkhu and M.R. Kukrit Pramoj, the Buddhist monk maintained that *santosa* and *sunyata* are noble and constructive attitudes fully compatible with the requirements of modern life, but he was never able to convince the pragmatic M.R. Kukrit. For all practical purposes it appears that government policy-makers and administrators will decide the acceptable contents of Buddhism in Thailand's schools.

The influence the state has on religious education appears clearly in the current curriculum, that was enacted in 1978. It is the lasting heritage of Prime Minister Thanin Kraiwichien (1976–77) who came to power in the counter-revolution of 1976, shortly after the 'fall' of Vietnam to communism and the unruly days of open democracy (1973–76). Proceeding from the old idea that the order of society follows from the individual conduct of its members, he wanted to strengthen the moral fibre of the nation. To this end, the subjects of good conduct, ethics and religion were to be given more prominence in (especially) elementary school education, at the expense of the more academic subjects. Accordingly, seventy-five percent of school time in the fifth and sixth grades is now devoted to the socialization of tractable subjects of the state.

The rewritten curriculum[2] did away with the explanation of merit-making ceremonies, sacred objects, the spirits and the gods, astrology, Buddha's life stories, nirwana, the next life, the *kathin* offering of new robes to the monks, amulets, dreams, and the other so-called animistic accretions that pervade Thai everyday life, and that were part and parcel of the earlier school-books. In its stead came the emphasis on paying obeisance to monks, and the teaching of Buddhist wisdom in the form of principles (*dhamma*'s) and proverbs. To lead an ethical life is to lead a quiet and a wise life, and thus meditation should be exercised and Buddhist wisdom needs to be understood.

Like always, the interesting question is: "Who does the explaining?" On the one hand, the influence of the teachings of Buddhadasa Bhikkhu is clear: no to *saksit* power and its seats, no to merit-making ceremonies, yet, his self-reliant intellectual interpretations naturally are at cross-purposes with those of the state. Thus, on the other hand, we find the influences of Thai elite culture and a hierarchically organized society that aim at instilling in the Thai child 'the qualities the nation desires'. As a result we find an interesting array of exhortations and explanations that are disguised as Buddhism but that actually reflect the requirements of official national culture.

This becomes quite apparent when we read that the Buddha taught people to be tractable, or docile *(wa non son ngai)*, to be orderly, to stick to the precepts, to be honest, and to come on time *(sic)*, while following the laws, rules and regulations of society, too. In other words, people who are religiously good will also be tractable subjects *(phonlamuang di)* who, through being so, contribute to the country's prosperity, stability and peacefulness. Thanks to religion, people can know what is right and wrong and hence, how to achieve a quiet existence together. They can rely on religion; it bolsters society and nation, it creates order and happiness. There are so many problems, suffering and unrest in the world these days, it is asserted, because people do not follow the tenets of their religion.

The stress on gratefulness and reciprocity stands out, so reinforcing the idea of the social nature of the human being. It is, therefore, not surprising that the idea of self-dependency is not pursued beyond the third grade. There, the main message is to be self-reliant in the execution of tasks and duties in order to please the parents and to demonstrate one's gratitude to them. Children should take care to refrain from making a nuisance of themselves. And with these emphases we are thoroughly back to Thai socialization rather than to Buddhist wisdom.

The fact that it is Thai culture that is being presented is very clear from the disparity in interpretations. According to orthodoxy, the saying 'Man depends upon himself' *(ton pen thiphung haeng ton)* is an exhortation to be self-dependent, to exercise and use one's own judgement and not to believe people because they are older, in authority or presumably wiser. What's more, people should certainly not place their faith in the spirits and the gods. It is obvious, though, that this orthodox view disagrees with the way Thai society is supposed to function. So, by recasting Buddhism to fit into the mould of the Thai ethos, a picture emerges that seamlessly integrates Buddhism in the construction of wider society, at the same time leaving no room for other types of Thai worship, even though there is occasional (unintended?) mention of them. Buddhism is presented as endorsing a hierarchical society with its demands of gratefulness, obligation, obedience, rote-learning, desire for disciplined subjects and (national) stability. In short, an interesting mixture of Buddhadasa Bhikkhu's message and the requirements of the state (For elaboration, see Mulder 1997: ch. 1).

Whatever the shortcomings of the mandatory school texts, there are also three grades of *naktham*, or 'Dhamma expert' courses for the formal study of Buddhism. This curriculum was designed early in this century and serves to instruct interested monks and laymen. The method of instruction relies heavily on rote-learning, and although all of the essential Buddhist concepts occur, many explanations are summary and relate neither to practical nor to deep Buddhism. In the instruction for the highest Dhamma diploma one finds, for instance, considerable information about meditation, but mostly consisting of names of methods and stages. What meditation is all about— its psychology, its purposes, and how to practise—are not explained at all. To get to know something about the essence of Buddhism one needs an understanding teacher, but such understanding is neither a social nor a formal religious requirement. Moreover, good teachers are rare and difficult to find.[3]

Memorization for the sake of having knowledge or the narrowly defined school-room Buddhism for the sake of good citizenship both suffice in the old Thai conception of knowledge: knowledge is a frozen Dharmasastra, that is, a fully developed yet static system of the right formulae and the appropriate rules. Knowing a Pali text does not imply a need to understand it, but one has acquired knowledge of a sacred, magical formula that fits certain ritual occasions. Knowing the formal rules of good behaviour is enough to ensure that one will behave well. The Thai system of moral education is fixed, and the repetition of the formulae and rules is thought to create auspiciousness and morality in society. Every Thai is familiar with the proverb, "Do good, receive good; do evil, receive evil" which explains the Law of Karma, but the present generation is not content with the idea of karmic retribution over many lifetimes into eternity, but rather wants to know why it is now experiencing so many contraventions of this rule; formal instruction—whether in temple or in school—never trains students to understand the discrepancies between theory and practice. While sharing in the fund of common Buddhist lore creates a unity of culture, the individual requirements for harmonious communality in modern times demand a deeper understanding and, even more, a critical attitude towards the role of Buddhism in coping with changes from within the country and without.

Modernity means criticism: reformers and identity

The overall picture of the state of conventional religion is not to the liking of all Thais. It is especially those intellectuals and monks who worry about secularization and traditionalism who would like to bring new relevance to the old heritage. They fear that the ossification and placidity of institutionalized Buddhism will further its growing irrelevance in the moral life of the nation and relegate it to a place in folklore as a colourful tradition, as a kind of embellished animism, while its moral message will decline and be increasingly misunderstood. What reformers and critics want is a revitalized and essential Buddhism replete with messages relevant to modern times. They want to cleanse the practice of Buddhism of archaic superstitions, of animistic accretions, of ritualization and magical practices. They want to shake up the sleepy and complacent hierarchy and are irritated at many monks' preoccupation with titles and honour in a rigid hierarchy of ceremonialism and self-indulgence. Critics want to free the monkhood of its political functions and identification with the establishment, especially in its higher ranks, and they want the Sangha to be independent. They would like to rewrite the Buddhist curricula and to bring Buddhism to life by instilling its timeless message. Moreover, they would like to see the active involvement of monks in the physical welfare of the population. In short, dissenters want to reform and reorient the ancient religious heritage.

To most Thais the critics' message is shocking; Thais have always thought themselves to be good Buddhists and now they suddenly have to hear that they are not and that their beliefs, practices, and rituals—as well as the institution that they venerate as sacred and inviolate—are all mistaken. Laymen are told that they have to personally reflect about the traditions that they have always taken for granted. Necessarily they feel threatened in their identity feelings and are not pleased.

While movements for religious reform are no novelty in Thailand, the present impulses are interestingly different from older, most often politically or administratively inspired reform movements. Since near the beginning of the present dynasty in 1782, the Buddhist cannon has been translated and standardized in order to have one authoritative and impeccable Tripitaka as the holy book. There have also been various attempts to purify the monkhood in matters of discipline and ritual. Since early this century, the Sangha has been increasingly brought under a unified, centralized system of ecclesiastical law and national standards for Buddhist learning. All these codifications, however, concern the discipline of the monks and ritual purity as an end to itself; they fail to reach the matters of content and practice that the reform-oriented Buddhists criticize. Critics rather see the preoccupation with formality and ritual correctness to be an impediment to real spiritual reform. While the voices of such would-be reformers could have been heard much earlier, their intentions and criticisms became most widely visible during the three years of open society from 1973–76.

To most Thais the Sangha is a holy institution that is beyond the criticism of laymen. Such criticism is dangerous because it is sacrilegious, and thus inauspicious. The monkhood is superior to laymen, and even if certain monks lapse into human weaknesses, they are still the providers of necessary ritual and enable the making of merit. While many laymen know about the failure of some monks to maintain the monastic discipline, the average Thai considers that criticism should remain an internal Sangha affair and the laity should close their eyes to abuses. Laymen who are not that tolerant should be condemned.

Interestingly, though, criticism towards the Sangha has lately been most vocally expressed by monks and ex-monks, most of them graduates of the Buddhist universities. In 1972, a very high-ranking monk published *The*

Way to Wake up the Monks[4] that saw three printings within two years. This book is a description of—and a vehement attack against—corruption, malpractices, and inefficiency in the highest Sangha circles and also criticizes the practice of magic, esotericism and superstition among senior monks.

In his collected writings, *Buddhism, Society, and Politics* (1977)[5] another high ranking ex-monk blasts the preoccupation with rank, titles, and honours in the higher Sangha circles, and argues the relevance of Buddhism for modern society. In 1976, there even appeared a biweekly periodical, *The Voice of the Young Sangha* that attacked the abuses within the Buddhist hierarchy while urging for openness, efficiency, and independence in the Sangha administration, for the opening up of relevant positions for bright young monks, and for new ideas and a measure of democracy within the stultified hierarchy.

With *The Wisdom of Thai Education* (in Thai, 1975), the monk-scholar-administrator Phra Rajavaramuni published one of the best critical analyses of modern Thai society. He correlates the weaknesses of the monkhood with those of society. One of his key arguments is that Thai society has lost its cultural direction: it has too readily abandoned its old and deeply rooted values and institutions for a process of aping the West. Modern Thai society has developed a fascination with materialism and the outward symbols of modernization but these are neither understood nor effectively incorporated in the new style of life that is characterized by the growing gulf between the haves and the have-nots. In the process, the masses now lack effective cultural leadership while the 'modern' leading class lacks direction; at the same time the elite has forgotten the function, role and usefulness of a viable monkhood in Thai society. Phra Rajavaramuni strongly stresses the neglect of the Sangha's educational function and argues that the government spends more money to provide a bachelor's degree for one hundred sons and daughters of the upper and middle classes than to educate the almost 200,000 young Sangha members of a poor rural background who depend on the Sangha for their education.

Another learned ex-monk, Achan Saeng Chan-ngam, published the article, "The Monkhood in Present-day Society" (in Thai, 1977), in which he discusses the weaknesses of the monkhood in terms of its tasks. These tasks are (1) to teach the Buddha Dhamma; (2) to practise the Dhamma and follow the discipline; (3) to stimulate the development of the Sangha and of lay society; (4) to be counsellors to the people. He sees inadequacies in the fulfilment of the first two tasks, which constitute the paramount duty of the monks. To teach or practise the Dhamma in a modern, relevant way, Sangha members should understand the Dhamma, its practice, and its relevance first of all. Achan Saeng, however, is pessimistic that this basic condition can be fulfilled given the ossified and conservative structures of hierarchy and education. In order to stimulate the relevance of monks in present-day society, he therefore suggests that monks should be trained for development work and for understanding the variety of modern problems that beset the common citizen, thus enabling monks to contribute to their solution.

These latter suggestions of monks doing social work also abound in laymen's publications that usually shy away from direct criticism of the monkhood but still want to capitalize on its traditional prestige. Such publications often suggest that this prestige should be channelled towards modern leadership and expressed in community development activities inspired by Buddhism (in contrast to engaging in similar activities for the sake of the state). These laymen's publications are numerous, indicating the living interest of a substantial, mostly intellectual and modern, segment of the population in maintaining a role for Buddhism in modern society; they also emphasize the need for in-depth understanding of the Buddha Dhamma and the practice of meditation, an interest apparently also alive among certain groups of university students. In 1974, students at Thammasat University organized an interesting conference on the role of Buddhism in modern society under the provocative title "Operating upon the Buddhist Religion". This title in itself assured that the proceedings of the conference were to land on the list of banned books under the Thanin Kraiwichin government.

Be this as it may, many publications by laymen and monks alike propagate the saving of Thai society from its indirection and the excesses of modernization by a return to the pristine values and truths of Buddhism. Most prominent among these are the works of the late Buddhist thinker and reformer of Wat Suan Mok in Chaiya,[6] the venerable Buddhadasa Bhikkhu, who directed his criticism not so much against a stultified hierarchy in which he did not believe, but at the fallacies of lay practice and inappropriate lay demands that, according to him, characterize the debased quality of Thai Buddhism. Buddhadasa argues that Thai Buddhism is a superstitious practice, that conventional merit-making is a mechanical contract for buying oneself a good rebirth, and thus about as "useless as raising chickens in order to feed the eggs to the dogs". His strong language did little to enhance his popularity beyond the small group of reform-minded intellectuals. Yet Buddhadasa's thinking and interpretation of Buddhism is certainly one of the most enlightened and penetrating that has ever been produced in Thailand. But the question is: Who, in an expanding consumer society, is interested in enlightenment?

Current trends

When we take a look at the contemporary religious scene, we may discern a variety of developments. Buddhadasa-inspired rational Buddhism remains influential among urban intellectuals; tradition- and power-oriented practices are as vital as ever, and coalesce in the new middle class-based cults; others set on serious ethical and religious practice, such as the Santi Asoke sect; others still feel attracted to the discipline and esoteric meditation of the Thammakai movement. For a long while, the urban intellectuals were the most conspicuous group. They are the people who want to bring modern relevance to old practices, they identify with both Buddhism and 'Thai-ness', and they are uneasy about this identification in modern times. Most often they appear to be the same urban intellectuals and social critics who also worry about the other problems that beset Thai society, the physician Prawet Wasi being an prime example.

The reform-oriented intellectuals constitute a tiny minority that serves as an irritant to all those others who also call themselves Buddhists, and who, if they publish, readily accuse the reformers of disrespect or even sacrilege and heresy. To these conventional believers, who constitute the vast majority, Buddhism is a way of life, an identity, and the key to primordial Thai-ness. Any protest, any attack, on their religious feelings touches a raw nerve. According to their understanding of the Buddhist faith, they are just as good Buddhists as the reformers. They are right, since orthodox sources define that (Buddhist) faith as belief in Karma; in the results of Karma; in the fact that karma originates from one's personal actions; alongside belief in the enlightenment of the Buddha. By these criteria well over ninety percent of the Thais are nominally Buddhists. The non-reformers, therefore, feel attacked if a small minority of mainly intellectuals tells them that they are inferior and mistaken Buddhists, and that their identity-maintaining practices and beliefs are *ipso facto* mistaken as well. To them Buddhism is a way of life and, whether mingled with animism or not, a means of sacred protection and auspiciousness in an unruly world.

The tradition-oriented people are not interested in spiritual or intellectual depth but rather in survival. To them religion offers protection and security in a world in flux, a thing to cling to, not for the sake of a religious way of life but as an identity and a means towards blessing. With the onset of modernity and its profound social changes, animistic expressions of religion are flourishing and apparently on the increase, with more and more magically gifted monks producing amulets, holy water and the like; with cults venerating potent images and shrines; and other practices aimed at good luck and supernatural blessing. Monks will respond to this overwhelming social demand if they want to maintain their popularity, such as exemplified by the very venerable Luang Pho Khun Parisutho of Wat Banrai who is not only renown among national politicians seeking his blessing, but who has even been honoured by the King visiting his temple (11 January 1995). On this occasion, the monk presented the royal charities the neat sum of seventy-two million baht, accumulated by the production and 'letting' of much sought after amulets.

Amulets and mantras are not on their way out, and shamans and charismatic monks mediate between sacred power and the laity, including big businessmen and politicians. Most interesting is the current vogue of cults among members of the urban middle classes. As a source of comfort in the confusion of modern life, the devotion to the Chinese goddess Kuan Yin enjoys a new, spreading popularity. The spectacular expansion of the cult of the Fifth Reign (King Chulalongkorn) seems to have captivated the imagination of all involved in commerce and trade, as this devotion is reputed to bring in business and money. Presently, many hold the spirit of the fifth king to be the equivalent of the guardian spirit of the country, that is, the *sayam-thewathirat*.

Next to these, one finds the moral reform-oriented Santi Asoke sect that combines a moderate, vegetarian style of life with ecological consciousness as the means to maintain one's mental health in this time of materialistic, capitalist development. Yet, the appeal of a moral way of life is not drawing in the crowd, while the combination of discipline and esotericism offered by the exceedingly prosperous Thammakai sect attracts the younger members of the middle classes by droves. Both sects propagate essentially individual-centred messages, one emphasizing the importance of personal moral behaviour, the other the acquisition of individual potency.[7] It may very well be that these concur with the current social evolution that brings to the fore the experience of urban anonymity and the unauthentic identity symbols offered by mass consumer culture. The respective stresses on moralism and meditation contrast with the prewar, and still socially optimistic, message of wisdom and intellectual development of Buddhadasa Bhikkhu. While his somewhat elitist message remains influential among people discussing religious reform and social reconstruction, it does not connect well with the experience of those striving for survival and an external hold in life.

THE IDEOLOGY OF 'DEMOCRATIC GOVERNMENT HEADED BY THE KING'

This chapter contains an analysis of how the public world, or the wider society beyond early, essentially private, familial-communal experiences, is introduced at elementary school. It is there that some basic skills, such as the three R's, and images of history and society, are transmitted. I shall focus on the latter, inasmuch as they are contained in the current books (1990s) aiming to prepare the student for participation in wider social life.[1] Such school texts are a very important part of the culture of the nation-state, reflective of the 'dominant mentality', at least as seen and interpreted by government and bureaucracy. Because of this, the Department of Education exercises strict control over textbook content and considerable influence over the actual presentation of the curriculum.

The three institutions—Nation-Religion-King—integrating history, society, and people

The history that the school-books project is royal history: without 'King', there is no Thailand, and there would be no 'Nation'. In this view there is no place for ordinary people, and chronological history stops short in 2475/ 1932, or in 1934 at the latest, when the seventh king stepped down from the throne. While it is true that there has been nominal kingship all the time, a discussion of the 'republican-democratic' period (1932–1957)— mainly under military strongman Marshal Phibun Songkhram—and of develop-ment since than, is totally avoided. As a result, the better part of the twentieth century remains without actors. This period is presided over by the present King who is represented as a father of the people, as one who takes their problems to heart. His wisdom and kindness offer relief from misery and natural adversity. Such as it is reiterated of all kings, this places the history-less and face-less commoners in a dependent relationship of gratefulness and obligation. Without 'King', there is no 'Nation'; without a leader, the Thais are nobody.

'The people' appear as an undifferentiated whole. There is no social structure, and it is only incidentally that the reader learns about slavery and a class of privileged lords and masters. On the whole, though, 'Nation' is an anonymous mass, alternately equated with the Thais (*khon thai; chao thai*), the country and nation (*prathet; prathet-chat; chat banmuang*), the people (*prachachon; ratsadon; phonlamuang*), society (*sangkhom*), state (*rat*), and the common interest (*prayot suanruam; satharana prayot*). This populace is the recipient of exalted goodness and, therefore, under the obligation of being good themselves. How to be good is taught by the fountain-head of moral guidance, namely, 'Religion', which in practice means the official interpretation of Buddhism. This explains why the Buddha is said to have instructed that people must be tractable, solve their own problems ('independent'), be obedient to the government, come on time, and feel grateful and indebted to Nation-Religion-King. Besides, 'the people' is presented as a homogeneous mass which is child-like relative to its leaders; thus the populace is clearly in need of the moral guidance of monarchs, elders, officials, and monks lest they stray aimlessly in the wilderness.

'Nation' is the most dependent of the Three Institutions; it is at the bottom of the pile, just like in the European Middle Ages when the estate of the Nobility tried to lord it over those of Religion and People. But whereas in the western situation the Church was a most formidable opponent of kaisers and kings (with all of them losing much of their power when emancipated urban middle classes—People/Nation—emerged during Renaissance and Reformation), there is no doubt that in Thailand, 'Religion' has always been under royal patronage, and that 'Nation' is considered as a dependent creation of kingship.

So, looking at the three 'estates' that compose the national ideology, it would almost seem as if they all fuse in 'King', that is, in a unitary nation that is defined by morality more than by borders, law, political economy, or body politic. Altogether this projects a static and eternal image, leaving no room for the analysis of social and economic structures, or of change, let alone the emergence and emancipation of the commoners as middle classes, or their demands on 'the system', such as education; a constitution; democracy; enterprise; control over government and bureaucracy. Especially in relation to the recent past, say, since the Bowring Treaty, the dynamics of Thai history and society become incomprehensible because they are not historically and sociologically presented but cast in a moral mould that blurs all distinctions.

Society as a moral construct

The moralizing image of society offered in school is rather simplistic: you either belong to it, or not at all. The task of the school is to produce morally good people (*khon di*) that are determined by a rather simple-minded set of values. In the family, people are taught to be diligent and perseverant, tolerant and exercising self-restraint, helpful and economical, possessed by responsibility and a sense of duty while giving way to others. As children, they must also be obedient. Such are the qualities of morally good people.

Primary school adds the values of discipline, self-mastery, (moral) knowledge, and sound reasoning. Those who demonstrate these values will qualify as good people. Being good is a safeguard against individual loss of face and also promotes the reputation of the group; if everybody behaves accordingly, family, school, community, and society will be peaceful and free of trouble.

In a black-and-white fashion, 'good' is constantly contrasted with 'bad'. Good leads to the rewards of acceptance, love, admiration, and contentment; bad to negative experiences, upset, loss of love and goods, yes, even to ill health and death. Basically the choice is with individuals, but seen morally it is not a choice at all, because people are obliged to be good since they are members of families and schools, that is, children of parents and pupils of teachers. This entails that they must reciprocate the goodness received, and this is achieved by being good.

Because of the steady emphasis on goodness received, gratefulness and obligation to reciprocate appear as the cardinal principles of the social construct. As this obligation is also due to increasingly vaguer and more distant entities such as community, country-and-people (*prathetchat*), and the Three Institutions, moral ties are extended to include all and sundry within the kingdom's borders. That totality is presented as a homogeneous collectivity of people that is 'encompassed' by its indebtedness to the supreme goodness of 'King'. In this view there is no place for structural oppositions (e.g., rich-poor; privileged-disadvantaged), let alone for conflict. By stressing the good while rejecting the undesirable, the moral model offered in school does not deal with society in any real sense, but depicts a utopian community.

This projection of what is basically a theory of the moral, functionally integrated, solidary family into the wider society, the public sphere and the nation, naturally extends familial duties to the nation-state. Hence, its subjects are required to be usefully occupied, not just taking care of themselves, but also contributing to the common welfare. Together with this, the functional representation of tasks and duties—all work is honourable and useful, whether as a doctor, policeman, or street-sweeper—makes it possible to present society as a seamlessly integrated, structureless whole, in which differences in prestige, power, position, and opportunity, are totally negated.

Seen from the perspective of the moral family, this is irrelevant: if something is good for daddy—for instance, to earn himself a pile of money —it must be good for the children as well, and so in wider society the (corporate) boss cannot go wrong. Also, in terms of giving moral guidance, father has the final word, and his authoritarianism cannot but be for the benefit of his dependents. Thus teachers, headmen, commanders, or prime ministers obviously speak rightfully, and should be trusted. As patrons they can only have the good of all in mind.

It should be clear that this conception has the potential of terrorizing the individual subjects of a state: they have functionally integrated obligations that construct the whole, thus contributing to its well-being. They should, therefore, shut up and do their work, which equates with fulfilling their moral task and duty, with being 'good people', and so it does not come as a surprise that the words 'role and duty' are commonplace throughout the texts whereas the word 'right' only occurs in connexion with voting.

The origin of democracy

In the discussion of the Seventh Reign, the King is said to have anticipated the demand for popular participation in government. In principle, he was in favour of instituting democracy, but he was held back by the grandees of the realm who held that the population at large was not ripe for it. So, basically, he was a modern monarch and a democrat, willing to allow the people to participate in government. His good intentions were pre-empted by the coup d'état of the People's Council of 24 June 1932.

The reasons given for the coup are: foreign-educated Thais had come into contact with European democracy; the inspiration of the examples set by the Chinese, Japanese, and Turkish revolutions; the economic crisis; the role of the press in leading the public to detest the government; the fact that absolute monarchy was behind the times; and finally, the feeling amongst the ordinary people that the privileged under absolute rule had too much power—which increased the distance between the (two) classes of the population. Be these reasons as they may, the tangible results of the coup were the establishment of a government of (mainly) commoners, and the fact that the King, on the tenth of December that year, graciously bestowed a constitution upon the Thai people (ETB, *Country*:115–21).

In the textbooks, important national days are classified in three clusters, to wit: religious, monarchical, and popular-traditional. My naivety was upset when I noted for the first time that Constitution Day is considered as a royal occasion. It is observed that (in the 'republican' times between 1932 and Marshal Sarit Thannarat, who began promoting the ideology of kingship again) Constitution Day (as the symbol of the emancipation of the commoners) was enthusiastically celebrated, country-wide, and on a big scale. Nowadays, however, "we have done away with that extravagance while gratefully remembering the superior goodness of the seventh king" (ETB, *People*:126–8). With this statement we come to the end of Thai history, the Seventh Reign being the last to be known by concrete dates and deeds.

Myth-making

At this point in the narrative, state ideology, or mythology, takes over, with the king hovering over the country while sending down a steady stream of blessings. The texts focus attention on the monarch's interest in the welfare of the villagers and other suffering people (Red Cross; wounded soldiers); the royal development programmes in the hills and mountains; agriculture, artificial rain, water projects, and school-building (ETB 4:186–96). The sixth-grade reading material (ETB, *Country*:101–9) adds to this: the king's important role as the patron of religion; the good luck of the Thai people of having a centre of unity in the monarch; the function of the king as a cherished, protective guardian (*mingkhwan*) of the people; and his unifying role, that enables the people to feel that they are one family (ETB, *Country*:106–7). This chapter also dwells on the constitutional position of the ruler, who is in a 'sacred' position (*thi sakkara*) and exercises sovereign power in the name of the people. As a result of his goodness and position, the Thai people should demonstrate their loyalty to him by showing their respect, by fulfilling their obligations, and by living according to the royal teachings that emphasize honesty and justice, emotional self-mastery, patience and self-restraint, while abstaining from what is bad and devoting oneself to the common weal; all this will result in a stable and properous nation.

One way or another, this has always been the case, even under the most rigid absolutism:

> That the kings of the Ayutthayan period were very powerful, is true, but there was also the tradition of the king being held in check by the Ten Dhammas of the King and their firm belief in the Buddhist teachings. Because of these the king administered people and realm in such a way that people could live peacefully and happily. From time immemorial, the Thai kings have loved and been worried about the populace, as a father about his children. As a leader, the king has promoted the good and prosperity of the country so that the populace could always enjoy peacefulness and happiness. That is why we worship the institution of King forever. (ETB, 5:164)

A Thai point of view

In his essay, "Thailand: Nation and Country in Primary School Texts" (1995), the historian Nidhi Ieosiwong discusses various aspects of the contents of the school-books currently in use for the courses in Thai language and social studies, including history. In the context of his discussion, three points stand out. Inspired by Anderson's *Imagined Communities* (1983), professor Nidhi argues that the undifferentiated image of the nation-country that is consistently evoked in the school materials is that of an ideal family or village (47–88). Such an ideal, solidary community is naturally tied together by personalistic, moral bonds. According to his observations, it is this type of image of the nation and country that also prevails in the mass media, in local scholarly writing, in the administration's self-image, in art and in songs. It is held by all Thais, by simple people and professionals alike (86–8). If Achan Nidhi is correct in his opinion, it may be safe to conclude that the imagining of wider society along the lines suggested is a firm part of Thai (middle-class ?) culture.

Fully in line with our interests is his musing about the presentation of democracy in the books he consulted (79–83). His is a disgruntled discussion, in which he notes that even the origin of democracy is misrepresented (as it is in all the current textbooks) as a royal experiment of the Sixth Reign; then, however, the King had to reach the conclusion that the people were not ripe for it because of their lack of education. Be this as it may, at present there is democracy, and the books should explain it. Sorry to say, they concentrate on form more than on essence. Besides, the books stress the duties of the people while ignoring their rights in the democratic system. Basic rights and freedoms that the state cannot legally infringe upon, are never mentioned with the exception of the freedom of religion, which is introduced in such a way as to sound like a permission and not a basic right. The freedoms of expression, of association, of the own body, of property, and so forth, let alone the United Nations' basic human rights, are not mentioned at all.

Subsequently, the respected intellectual from Chiangmai University complains that the way democracy proceeds by frank and rational discussion of opposing opinions is misrepresented as a process of compromise and give-and-take; voting to seek majority opinion is avoided. This is similar to the way decisions are reached in villages where solidarity is the overriding goal. Resolute decision-making, such as voting on a class representative, is also side-stepped: the less worthy of the competing persons will withdraw from the race until the most appropriate person remains. All this apparently supports the old opinion that the Thai people still lack training in democratic decision making.

Finally he observes that the fact that democracy is about negotiating opposing opinions and interests is carefully kept from view by suggesting that decisions are taken in agreement with the interest and reputation of the (whole) nation. This image is fostered by equating the school with the nation, which is a serious distortion because life, and also the experience of the students, is much more diverse. The picture that emerges is that of national consensus under the inspired guidance of the country's royal administration (*ratchakan*); people who do not agree are made to appear as egoists. This way of presenting the issue fails to dwell on conflict resolution and ignores the question of the equality of citizens. To illustrate his points, Nidhi then highlights the distrust of democratic decision making by the way Singapore is presented in a school text:

> Because of its very resolute leadership, Singapore progresses. It has development planning that tightly integrates urban, population, educational, and employment development. The people of Singapore are very disciplined. (79–83)

A non-participant point of view

The books I consulted are partly the same ones as Achan Nidhi's, but while he focused on Thai and social studies, I looked at the materials that are considered to prepare one for life in society, such as ethics, social studies, and professional skills. This group of materials is held to be so important that it is allotted 75 per cent of the available school time in the last two grades.

The Ministry of Education is explicit about the purposes of primary education, stating that

> Primary education is that basic education that aims at developing the student in such a way that he can enhance the quality of life at the same time that he is useful to society in the sense of fulfilling his role and duties as a good member of the populace according to the democratic system of government headed by the King by giving the student the basic knowledge and skills for supporting social life and being abreast of change, to maintain good physical and psychological health, and to be able to work and seek a living in a peaceful manner.

CHAPTER 9

Further on, it is specified that students should

> have knowledge and understanding of social conditions and the societal change affecting home and community, to be able to behave according to role and duty as a good member of family and community while all the time taking care of and promoting the environment, religion, arts and culture in the community around the home (Kowit,1990: 5-9).

An important part of that knowledge and understanding consists of ethical rules, of being educated in good manners and correct conduct. These are summarized in the fifth grade. In a neat bureaucratic fashion, responsibility is specified in six clusters of duties, namely, the obligations to oneself, to the family, to the school class and fellows, to the school, to the community, and to the nation-state. All these are then specified in sets of four to seven rules to follow. For example, the duties to the nation-state are: 1) to respect the law; 2) to pay taxes; 3) to assist the officials in maintaining national stability; 4) to be loyal to and defend Nation-Religion-King; 5) to preserve national independence, Thai arts and culture, and to let the good of the nation prevail over self-interest (*Bunsong* 5:1–9).

It is against this background, and against the image of history and society the books project, that I want to present and comment upon the further statements made about democracy in the texts for the fifth and sixth grades. These are not awfully many, and I can thus present all of them. An interesting one is where the sixth King, Vajiravudh—popularly known as the Great Wise King—is credited with experimenting with democracy with his courtiers in order to guide the country to a level of progress equal to that enjoyed by the developed countries (ETB, *Country:*32).

> In the Seventh Reign, the Thais experienced the change of government towards democracy, albeit an incomplete one. Yet, already during the previous reign, the king experimented with democracy by establishing Dusit Thani, a hypothetical city for the purpose of trying out democracy. There was an executive branch of government, a constitution, elections, and everybody in that city was a commoner, including the king himself. Newspapers were published in which they could write critical articles and voice their opinions. The experiment resulted in the conclusion that the democratic system did

not yet agree with the situation of the Thai people because, at that time, they did not have sufficient education. Therefore, the king could not yet grant the people a democratic system of government and desired to make education available to the people in the first place. (*ibid.*:26–7)

Later on in the same book, we learn that it is because of the present King that the democratic system of government is firm and stable (108). This is followed by a formal scheme, devoid of elaboration, representing the three branches of government, in which parliamentary elections demonstrate that the population participates in government by way of representatives who execute their duties in agreement with the wishes of the people (110–1). About the People's Council it is still observed that its members studied abroad, where they noted systems of government and politics that granted the populace rights, freedoms, and participation in the country's administration (115). Yet, subsequently, we never hear about rights, freedoms, and participation again: the last relevant chapter consistently emphasizes the duties and obligations of the population—the word 'must' appearing in almost every sentence—while evoking the image that the people are there for the sake of the government, not the other way round (122–6).

The most explicit mention of a right, and what democracy is substantially about, occur in a passage at the end of a lengthy enumeration of all the duties of the Thai national.

There is another thing that people should do, but it seems that we do not think it to be important at all . . . Good denizens (*prachachon*) should use their right to elect people to run the affairs of the community who are honest and straightforward, with only the importance of the public good in mind. We should not be remiss of or indifferent to this right, because in our country we have a democratic system of government, in which the government is happy to listen to the opinions and the problems of the population. Because the population consists of so many people, we should elect people whom we trust to be good, who will work for the interest of community, society, and nation. Instead of all of us, it is these representatives who must inform the government about our opinion, our problems and suffering ... We should carefully consider the people who volunteer as representatives. Do they conduct themselves well all the time, do they devote themselves physically and mentally to their efforts in promoting the real progress of the community? We must elect only the best. (*ETB, People:*52–3)

Yet, the complaint that people are not serious about democracy and elect undeserving candidates in a world cut loose from its moral moorings becomes clear in the following passage.

When the teacher had finished explaining, Wibun asked 'Sir, they say that present-day people have almost no ethics, no [moral] reasoning, and no sense of justice. Do you agree, Sir?'
'I think I have to agree, although it is not so that this applies to everybody. In wider society we shall inevitably find that good and bad people mix. At present the number of people has risen while the level of material prosperity has gone up much less; mentality and ethical behaviour seem to be deteriorating. So, people compete for resources; they almost never enter the temple, and everyday they grow more distant from religion, unlike in earlier days. In a variety of ways, clever people try to take advantage of those who are ignorant or in a lower position. Sometimes they do not use their common sense, just following their emotions. People who have power, influence, or go against the law, do think themselves to be worthy people. This is why society is confused. If we assist each other in totally eradicating that type of people by not praising and admiring them, and by not electing them to parliament, we will be able to construct righteousness in social life'. (*ETB* 5:83–4)

Comments

Although some information about democracy is given in the texts, its basic ideas fail to come to life, and it never becomes a means to negotiate ideas and conflicts of interests between groups. In the second to the last quotation, the government is not presented in a democratic way, meaning, as a government of, for, and by the people. Quite the contrary, the government appears as an authority benevolent enough to listen to the people under its sway. All the time the words 'the people' and 'the public good' are used in a manner as if they were indivisible and clear entities, and in doing so, their meaning is thoroughly mystified. I do not think this is indicative of a conscious strategy to mislead the pupils: the inability to explain what democracy is, is related to a certain way of seeing society which blinkers the more distant, sociology-oriented way of looking at it. This needs some explanation.

I think I agree with Achan Nidhi that it is not just the school-books that look at Thai society in a certain way. People look at, and academic columnists comment upon, Thai society as if it were a community modelled after the family. Such a view is necessarily hierarchical, functional, and moralistic. To it belongs the idea that, if everybody fulfils 'role and duty' according to the demands of his relative (unequal) position, society will be well-ordered, stable, and quiet. Such a society is a moral construct in the first place, in which relationships, and the obligations they contain, are seen in a concrete, that is, a personalistic and particularistic way. As a result, the texts are fully consistent in equating society with community with nation with nation-state with the population with the public interest, and so on. This type of social imagination is not only incompatible with substantial democracy; it even makes it unthinkable.

Democracy is closely related to the ideal of fundamental human equality which subsequently entails the recognition of the moral autonomy of the individual and his basic rights and freedoms, even in the teeth of the demands of collectivities, such as group or state. Since equality and rights are never ceded for free, striving for emancipation becomes an imperative. This vision of desirable social change necessitates the sociological imagination that comprehends the human situation as conditioned by abstract structures and forces. Politically, this holds the possibility for democratic systems to arise in which political platforms direct the ways in which to construct society. The means of constructing society are not only found in rational debate, but especially in law, that is, in a depersonalized system to regulate society-in-the-abstract.

I do not think that the personalistic and moralistic social imagination is going to yield anytime soon in favour of the sociological and democratic one. I do not see any good reasons why it would, even if the former view is inadequate to comprehend, let alone regulate, the independent subsystems of state and economy. The latter two, as expanding fields of power, go by their own expedient rules and are not really waiting for the interference of a democratically organized civil society to define their limits and ways of operation, and so, seen from the point of view of the teacher in the last quotation, or from that of the wholesome family-community-nation for that matter, the wider world of society appears as an unruly realm where, in spite, or rather because, of the school's efforts, people lack effective moral guidelines. It may thus be that there is something to say for the Great Wise King's opinion after all.

THE UNDERSTANDING OF DEMOCRACY AND HUMAN RIGHTS

The skyscraping city-scape of Bangkok is emblematic of the social sea change of the past thirty or forty years. Even if, temporarily, the high-rising boom seems to have reached its limit, there can be no doubt that, in pace with urbanization and new economic circumstances, a new type of society came into being. Modernity was seeking its shape, and left behind it older, more 'predictable' arrangements. People went to school, learned new professions. Media expanded dramatically. Communication intensified at the same time that people became distant from and anonymous to each other. Relationships turned businesslike, money became their measure. People 'individualized'. They became consumers, too.

It is not to the point to detail the obvious, to note precisely how, in thirty years time, pedestrian traffic turned into fuming urban gridlock, how leisure turned into haste, how higher education became a mass industry. Suffice it to note that modernity brought new people to the fore, *homini novi*, ranging from factory labour to the often incredibly affluent nouveaux riches, and all those who are loosely referred to as the new middle classes. While there is no denying that there are recognizable continuities in this momentous transition, much is also changing unpredictably and beyond recognition. Mentality is being transformed as well.

One of the great challenges of these times is to build a culture adequate to respond to their exigencies. What we see is new people facing new circumstances for which they are ill-prepared. The moralistic advice they received during their school days is blatantly out of date. They have not been trained to reflect upon social and political questions. In other words, civilian debate and critical public opinion are still in their infancy; a civil society of consequence still needs to be built. Yet, culture is being created. New thinking is in the making.

Beginning in the 1980s, and especially after the Suchinda coup of 1991, debates opened up Thai public opinion. Discussions on all sorts of issues—ranging from the role of the military to women's lib, and from land reform to environmental problems—have enlivened the public discourse that was further animated by theinput of NGOs. The fifteenth and sixteenth constitutions were the subject of prolonged exchanges. Academic opinion-page writers lent sense and substance to the debates. Phone-in shows enticed the public to disagree and 'to look at things from a different angle'. Human rights and the question of justice were regular fare. Peasant protest and empowerment of the poor became acceptable, organizing seminars on any problem fashionable.

While all this is evident and heartening, it is not so clear yet whether an influential public opinion is being formed, whether a resolute civil society is being born, and whether informed views developed among the nation's intelligentsia are wielding influence in the world of political and corporate decision making. So, whereas some of the basic conditions of establishing a civil society, such as economically independent middle classes, the freedoms of association and expression, widespread formal education and an informed public, are in place, there remain good reasons to be wary about the prospects of a democratic mentality and way of life developing.

In Thailand, these conditions are undermined by the persistence of traditional politics. By this I mean the close alliance of business and the affairs of state; the absence of clear-cut party programmes; the *ad hoc* groupings of political entrepreneurs in expedient parties. Another debilitating factor is the newness of the urban middle classes, the members of which are mass educated, consumer culture oriented, socially inattentive, and interested in personal progress rather than in public problems. These attitudes may be reinforced by the older view that sees 'public' affairs as the concern of state and government in relation to which ordinary people are subjects rather than citizens. A further reason, as we noted in the previous chapter, is the way in which people learn to think about the public world. Have ideas like 'autonomous citizens', 'autonomy in opposition to the state', and participation in public affairs—essential ingredients of democratic citizenship—already penetrated the imagination?

Although expectations to the contrary have repeatedly been expressed, the newly educated urban middle classes seem less than enthusiastic, lukewarm at best, in their acceptance of the western ideas of participatory democracy and human rights. Voter turnout is low, newspaper discussions are moralistic rather than inspiring, while the press offers a dismal and cynical picture of political practice and the behaviour of 'traditional' politicians. Corruption seems to be the order of the day, while the instruments of state do not appear to be very much impressed by the policies—if any— formulated by the elected 'representatives of the people'. As a result, and in spite of the trappings of procedural democracy, the exercise of power is all too reminiscent of that of the strong centre of the days gone by, with the important difference of more people pulling or trying to pull the strings (chapter 1). Yet, the presence of many parties and interest groups in the modern political arena, and the frequent changes of government, have not made the political process more transparent than in the days of 'closed' and more exclusive politics. Participatory democracy remains hard to imagine, although the public apparently enjoys watching, discussing, and ridiculing the spectacle provided by confrontational politics.

Localization

To understand the attitude of the people toward democracy and human rights, we should situate their political culture within their social imagination. How do they think about social life and how do they perceive wider society? After all, it is to their view of social life that a foreign idea, such as democracy, needs to be adapted. This accommodation can best be viewed in terms of the theory of localization that holds that, in order to thrive, foreign elements need to be grafted on to a local stem; they will need to feed on local sap in order to develop and flourish. In other words, they will not spontaneously fit in with the new environment, but need to fuse with it, in the process acquiring local content and meaning. The new local environment will redefine their characteristics, but at the same time it will itself be changed somewhat by the adoption of, or exposure to, these new elements.

Because an idea generally comes in a package of related ideas, we normally find that some of them readily secure a local stem, and then evolve into the image of the receiving culture, while others fail to connect and to develop local meaning. For instance, Thai religion is future-oriented and preoccupied with seeking blessing and auspiciousness, potency and efficaciousness, in the here and now (chapter 2). As a result, sources of the latter could easily be appropriated, and charismatic monks, merit-making, the worship of power-laden statues of Buddha, the cult of relics and amulets, potent rituals and sacred texts could feed and flourish on native lifeblood. Conversely, ideas about liberation, basic moral equality and individual autonomy, although 'physically' present, remained peripheral to culture and practice.

In a similar vein, we must evaluate how people think about the public world of wider society, and how the democratic process, legality, and human rights—as institutions by means of which civil society regulates that public world—fit in with existing ideas. By the public world I mean society in the sociological sense of *Gesellschaft*, that is the wider society beyond family and community where people are mutually anonymous and where they interact in a businesslike way. In the case of Thailand, I doubt whether the idea of a public world is felicitous. There, a public world of the public has never existed, the recent introduction of democracy—and its hand-maiden: a free press—notwithstanding. What existed, at best, was the theatre state, visible to all, yet monopolized by the political centre. When considering Thailand, it is perhaps preferable to talk about the 'external world of society'.

The image of the external world

There are two main images of the external world beyond community; one is the primordial world representing nature—the surrounding wilderness in opposition to settled life and civilization. It is nobody's and everybody's land, a field of opportunity to be appropriated as the need arises, but not one's responsibility, really. It is a shared resource, but not a common possession. This image is still important to understand behaviour vis-à-vis the external world, both in its natural and social aspects.

The second image is that of the dynastic realm, of a ruler uniting a diversity of local communities under his sway, claiming rights over all the land and its inhabitants. What is not held by community members or groups is considered to be 'of the king' (*khong luang*), the government, or a powerful, influential local godfather (*chaopho*). It is their 'private' space which they regulate and for which they are responsible; it is not 'of the public', the people, or the nation; hence it is not the public good.

This dynastic, pyramidal image of the external world as belonging to a paramount chief, who is seen as a superpatron to whom persons relate in a patrimonial fashion, is reminiscent of the order of the family, which is, after all, a place where moral inequality comes naturally. In a way, the family's arrangements and ideology are projected into the external world; they explain the ideal order of society and serve to construct its image.

The cardinal elements of this image are hierarchy, moral obligation, shared well-being, mutual dependence, and the recognition that individual members' identities are primarily defined by the group to which they belong; personhood is membership. This relational image makes for a very personalized conception of social life that, in combination with hierarchy, leads, by its own logic, to the idea of ethics as the ethics of place. If everybody behaves according to his (temporary) station in life, fulfilling its obligations, the family, community, and ultimately the external world of society, and thus the state, too, will be in desirable order.

Apart from the role of individual moral awareness, keeping society in good order is definitely the task of the government, culminating in a personalized leader, a 'man of prowess' capable of dominating the external world. He enforces desirable order, and what is good for him, as a father, should be good for all. It is, therefore, loyalty to him, and the collectivity he stands for, that is far more important than law as a means of maintaining good order. Consequently, the seeking of patronage defines political behaviour, while the group—nation, state, region, country, people—is seen and defined in moral rather than in legal terms; society is a moral construct.

Trust in hierarchy and loyalty to leadership are basically moral acts that agree with the highly personalized image of social life, in which the unknown areas of the external world are somewhat alarming and definitely awe-inspiring. In a way, it is like nature, filled with mysterious forces and spirits, but also a field of opportunity; socially it is the arena of competition for power and position of the grandees and bosses, often rather violent, where an unobtrusive little man may also appropriate an occasional prize.

It is this understanding of the external, 'public' world that provides the matrix in which the ideas of democracy and human rights must be localized. The identifying marks of that world appeared to be that it is not seen as a public trust but rather as a field of opportunity where people are concerned with their personal interests first of all. There the high and mighty claim their 'rights' and function as patrons vis-à-vis those in lesser positions. This 'personalizes' the external world, and makes it moral; it is seen in the familial terms of basic inequality and the ethics of place. Before we can dwell on the transformations this matrix causes to the ideas and practice of democracy and human rights, we should briefly consider the premises of the latter two.

Premises of democracy and human rights

In their self-proclaimed 'new world order', the Americans apparently push to institute 'free and fair elections' in all the countries of the world as a sign that democratic government prevails. Yet, democracy is part of a complex set of ideas; some of its related procedures are easily adopted, at the same time that its spirit and participatory practices fail to acquire local meaning.

The ideas of democracy and human rights stem from an environment that grounds morality in equality: individual people matter, they have a right to their opinion, are morally autonomous, and equal before the law; they have the right, and the duty, to be informed and to partake in the public discourse. Practically, this highlights the role and function of a free press, and implies the freedoms of expression and association, alongside the right to vote.

As a means of regulating wider society, democracy involves the people, thus making that society a public world. It sees that world in a sociological manner—as an abstract structure of institutions and power relationships, of conflicting interests and ideas, that are subsequently discussed in a frank fashion and that can be influenced by policy decisions and the implementation of law. Society is neither static, nor merely subject to contingent forces, but governable and constructable, most often in the name of the public interest or common good.

Transformations

It should be clear that the premises of democracy do not quite agree with the Thai image of the external world, and that their localization may therefore lead to interesting transformations and surprising outcomes. The picture that it yields is, of course, not a static one, and the ideas and practices surrounding democracy and human rights are perennially evolving in pace with the globalization of the world community, and very strongly so under the influence of the many tens of thousands of local intellectuals familiar with the West through many years of study. The following stock-taking, therefore, is nothing more than a summary overview of present political culture.

What we find is the existence of procedural democracy, meaning that certain, ostensibly democratic institutions—such as a constitution, parliament, elections, and laws—are in place. The problem is how they are animated and substantiated. Constitutions without the spirit of con-stitutionalism are modern documents that show the world that the country is 'civilized', yet they neither appear to refer to a moral consensus of the populace, nor are they exactly awe-inspiring. Thailand, with sixteen constitutions in sixty years, offers an excellent example of the 'patience of paper' and the tenuous connexion of basic laws with the ordering of the external world. And then, its parliament: what and who does it represent? Granted, some politicians have indeed been elected; others have been appointed, and the military is heavily represented. Yet, do they represent the people who elected them? Or the districts that voted them into power? Or the entity that appointed them? Do they stand for programmes or ideologies? Do the decisions and laws they issue really regulate life in the wider society?

The democratic institutions of Thailand are dominated by strong figures and their interest groups ('parties'), who sometimes have a clearly recognizable provincial basis. In a very personal and confrontational manner they work for their interests, and those of their factions, apparently equating their affairs with 'public affairs'. They offer a very competitive and often violent spectacle, are normally able to buy, or otherwise manipulate, the vote, and still excite the people enough to trigger off considerable political violence (Pasuk and Sungsidh, 1997). Yet, in reality, they offer neither plans nor programmes, though elected strongmen will see to it that money and projects to improve infrastructure are directed to their districts or provinces of origin.

The focus of the political process is with such godfathers who, if they become powerful prime ministers, may even preside over the country's affairs while sharing the benefits of their sway with their political, military and business cronies. Yet, in their rhetoric, they pose as visionary leaders who have the well-being of the nation at heart. In this way they confirm the dynastic image of the external world.

Popular culture surrounding the political process highlights the theatrical aspects of the nation-state. It is national events that stand out in the press, featuring the confrontations between prominent politicians representing themselves. Sarcastically referred to as 'the clowns', they provide a public show reminiscent of the cockfight to which the people figure as kibitzers and audience. Less confrontational but no less spectacular are the representations of politics as a national emblem in the electronic media, such as ministerial appearances, royal ceremonies, national celebrations, ritual discussions of and newscasts about political events, endless screening of national symbols—in short, the ingredients 'civic religion' is made of. Politics is spectacle.

Politics is about power, about laying claims on the external world; a contest for privilege and of setting the law. To understand the exercise of power, it is important to know how it is perceived. Power is an attribute of strong men, of 'men of prowess' who can impose their will on an unruly, an unlawful external world, enforcing their order there. In the modern context, that order is subject to the expedience of state and economy, which operate as independent systems of power (and competition). Their power operates in an area that is beyond the moral, consensual rules of the inner world of family and community, in an area that is 'anonymous' and businesslike. Such power is morally neutral. Of a politician, or a person in a privileged position, it is expected that he uses this power, for his own purposes, his benefit, and in the interest of those who depend upon him. As a result, the idea of corruption sits uneasily in the Thai context. The external world, like the forest, is there to be exploited; it is a shared resource, not the public good.

The moral model that is projected into the external world of nation-state-country-people-realm is that of the integral, cohesive family that subsumes its members, who are supposed to identify with and serve it. That model is strongly hierarchical and emphasizes consciousness of place, role, and obligation: it is these that seemingly define personhood. This is not only apparent from the teaching of civics in school, but also surfaces in the dogma that the family is the basic building block of society, and in the propagation of—nowadays often western, middle-class—family values as the redeemer of good society. While the image of the nation-state as family is ubiquitous, the reification of values as causes of desirable order is most tangibly expressed in the teaching going on at school and the philosophy that guides it. People are mutually unequal, have different roles and duties that they should faithfully execute because they are under obligation to the Three Institutions, that is to Nation-Religion-King. If everybody behaves accordingly, society, nation, and state cannot but be in the most desirable order. In other words, a peaceful and happy (*sa-ngopsuk*) society follows from the values individuals hold and their awareness of their ethical duty to their respective social positions.

Protesting people do not know or accept their place and role, their insolence perhaps even being based on the idea that they are as good as their leaders, that they are 'equals' in a moral sense and so can assert their causes. Such assumptions are more than threatening of the order that has hierarchy as its backbone: they are immoral. The point here is that the threat to order, or good society, is seen to originate from individual people who do not know how to behave, who do not possess *The Treasure of the Gentleman* (*Sombat khong phudi*; title of a famous school-book), and thus do not accept their place. This is also illustrated by the press that highlights the problems of having many poor people who go without schooling—and thus are not taught manners—who squat on valuable property, who invade protected forests, who violate the law, who gamble and get drunk. Individual poor people are the source of problems; the issue is seldom discussed as poverty.

Official political culture is, therefore, preoccupied with teaching morality. If all people know their manners and how to conduct themselves, the external world of wider society will be in good order. As a result, fifty to seventy-five per cent of primary school time goes to the teaching of how to be a good and tractable subject.

The emphasis on individual morality combines with the idea that values have agency of their own. As a result, abstract society is seen as an integral, functionally integrated, hierarchical family. This corresponds with, on the one hand, the old dynastic and moralistic model of the social order and hints, on the other, at the absence of a sociological view of society. It is not structures, institutions, and relationships that feature in (official) social thinking, but personal bonds, society being perceived as composed of subjective sets of moral obligations inhering in relationships. It is this view that also delineates political behaviour, the practice of 'democracy' and the understanding of human rights.

This dominant discourse is reflected in most of the press. Social affairs are moral issues and the avid reporting about politics highlights the confrontations and exploits of individual politicos. Apparently, most newspaper reportage is a commentary on the behaviour of prominent members of the national family, and although some incisive treatment of economic and financial matters can readily be found, structural social analysis is still scarce. As a result, the press, however critical of individual politicians, is only beginning to offer a modern discourse about democracy and public affairs and, in a situation where the abuse of justice is common, human rights issues are only commented upon when they are as spectacular as East Timor, the urban massacre of May 1992, the contempt of the military and the police for NGO-led rural protesters, or the constant harassment of the Burmese students having fled from the oppressive military dictatorship. Yet how such abuses sit with basic ideas about hierarchy and moral inequality, or with structure and process, remains obscure; the view of society as a moral construct blinkers such questions from view.

Discussion

Political culture—thinking about power and society—is part of the social imagination that is only slightly affected by the recent, twentieth-century supply of western ideas about regulating the external world. Like the community, the external world of wider society is seen in hierarchical, and thus moralistic terms and is, therefore, thought to respond to individual conduct and values education. Seen from such a familial, moral point of view, the modern outside world of politics and economy appears to be in moral decay; it constitutes a field of opportunity, too.

This perception is pervasive, and certain western-trained Thai social scientists still revert to moralistic analyses and recommendations when they address the problems of their own society, thus not only demonstrating their personal and emotional involvement, but also revealing the way in which they have been educated while at school in Thailand. This is often apparent in Thai newspaper commentary, although the debates triggered by the drafting of the 1997 constitution were remarkably more ideology-oriented, and may hint at a gradual maturing of Thai civil society. As a result, many, mainly urban, educated people now pin their hopes on the serious practice of democracy as a means to rein in traditional or godfather politics. Yet the hopes of the intelligentsia may experience a hard time in the face of persistent practice.

As a result, it hardly comes as a surprise that local conceptions about the ordering of the external world easily prevail. We witness the persistence of ideas about and practices related to hierarchical order, its positional ethics, leadership, privilege, patronage, and personalism. Yet the introduction of elections and 'representative' bodies has brought a new element to the regulation of intra-elite competition that, by its own logic, allows for the voicing of 'dissident' opinions and the articulation of new groupings, especially those representing economic interests, in the political centre. This means that politics gets more diversified, rather because of the diversification of the sources of power than because of democratization. The latter would more substantially be the case if political power were ceded to 'popular', 'participatory' influences, but present power-holders are not ceding more than elections and nominal representation; they remain traditional politicians.

A weird element—not introduced because of democracy, but rather because of the idea that politics is about regulating the public world, and very much used as offensive political ammunition—is the idea of corruption, meaning that the external world should not be exploited for personal gain, because it constitutes the public interest. This idea is so baffling that it lames all Anti-Corruption Commissions from the outset. The Thai vernacular expresses the idea of corruption by the European word, because nobody had apparently conceived of the practice before, and how could one if the external world is seen as a field of opportunity? The nearest equivalent the Thais could think of is the idea of *cho rat bang luang*, literally to defraud the populace and hide this act from the king, which refers to the practice of taxing, exploiting the people for the personal benefit of a tax-farmer or nobleman in excess of the royal stipulations—historically a normal practice known as *kin muang*—that does not carry the moral onus of unduly profiting from the common good.

It cannot be denied, however, that a certain basic ingredient of democracy and human rights is being promoted by the expansion of modern mass society, namely the fact of equality. In the new urban environment most people are unknown to each other, and anonymity means equality. Social order, with its relative positioning of actors, only arises when people transact in other than a businesslike manner. So, because mass society does not require the personalized elements of loyalty and solidarity, it generates an equality that may affect the experience and conceptualization of personhood. Persons, after all, find that they have more free space to move around in and develop themselves.

Whether factual equality and relative freedom will translate into the ideological demand for equality remains a moot point. While some may argue that the proliferation of NGOs and other ginger groups, environmentalist and feminist demands, and so on, are indicative of the development of a new political culture centring on participatory citizenship, others may point to the non-modern tendency towards moral particularism that expresses itself in such reactions against the anonymization of social life as familism, dogged individualism, religious revival and sectarianism, 'civic' club membership, and place of origin-based association. These latter manifestations of 'civil society' are parochial, that is, inward-directed, and befit the current evolution to an urban mass society that is indifferent to politics as long as the economy expands. In such an atmosphere, state and economy are not to be subdued by the weak demands for democratization and respect for human rights as expressed at the intellectual fringe of society.

The main argument here is that the idea of moral equality—fundamental to democracy and human rights—does not connect well with the Thai social imagination. Social order depends on hierarchy and respect for it is the ethical imperative; by its own logic it sees society as a moral construct. Because this view does not take distance, the wider society remains abstract and difficult to imagine. To govern that external world on the basis of equality is literally a far-fetched idea. Because of the absence of a practicable moral model of the external world, the expedient logic of state and economy will define how political affairs are run, and make for a 'traditional' political culture that involves the population as subjects at best. Legality exists on paper, but equality before the law is very weakly developed; the concept of human rights, let alone respect for them, is only vaguely understood, although people understand the idea of personal dignity—and respect for it —very well; (critical) sociological analysis is in its infancy, and a public world inhabited by morally autonomous citizens is not in the offing, other than in the visibility of small segments of civil society who push for democracy, administrative decentralization, social justice and civic rights. For the time being, such activists are marginal to the system and not represented in the centres of statist and corporate power.

The timeliness of political indifference

The activists referred to are basically the heirs of a culture of the public world that was developing among the generations of idealists who strove for social reconstruction and emancipation, for democracy and constitutionalism, roughly between the later days of royal absolutism and up to the agitated days of democratic experimentation (1973–76). At present, though, such ideas belong to the past and disagree with the culture of the public world that is evolving among members of the new urban middle classes, the bulk of whom are without a tradition of critical thinking about and participation in the public world. They are the product of a period of very rapid urbanization and equally rapid changes in the economic opportunity structure of the past thirty years. They differ qualitatively from the more exclusive middle group that studied when going to university was still a privilege, and whose members indulged in the luxury of thinking about democratization and social reconstruction. Most of the new people are upwardly mobile, mass-educated and oriented more towards professional advancement than to ideological musing. Besides, they acquired their skills during the period, beginning with the 1970s, of the systematic propagation of lifestyles and consumption. They grew up with television rather than with books.

Theirs is a culture of cynicism and indifference regarding the 'public' world of politics and the economy. Although they would like to see 'law-and-order' prevail, they tend to be socially inattentive; while suffering from the urban disorder they experience, they have no great ideas of how to improve it. This drives them to a stronger identification with family, friends, and other particularistic associations that emphasize individual worth.

Their individual-centred choices are made in the drive for self-improvement and careerism, and in the lifestyle phenomenon that, at the centre of consumer culture, enables people to accumulate the status symbols they need in order to assert their identity. These self-centred orientations lead away from ideological or theoretical attempts to come to grips with their public environment which, as a result, remains vague. As in the early days, they believe that personal ethical conduct is the wellspring of good society, while wider society appears as a field of opportunity where the individual carries little or no responsibility. It is everybody's and nobody's place, where people compete for scarce resources and where power is the most desirable commodity. As a result, only minimum demands on the public spheres of politics and the economy appear to be evolving, and so it seems that there is a general deficit of enthusiasm and idealism to promote 'substantial' democracy and human rights. In the contemporary Thai context, democracy remains procedural rather than substantial, at the same time that 'the duties of the subject' are better understood than 'citizens' rights'.

CONCLUSIONS

Thai society has for long been characterized by so-called loose structure, Buddhism, and individualism. The theory based on these concepts can be roughly stated as follows: the Thais are individualists because they are Buddhist; this is so because Buddhism teaches that one's karma and thus one's life is an individual responsibility; together these individualists make for a loosely structured social system where rules are flaunted and where considerable variation in individual behaviour is even positively sanctioned. At the high point of loose-structuralism, statements were made to the effect that 'Thai society always travels on the brink of social chaos' and that 'All Thai behaviour is set in a framework of cosmic impredictabilitie'. Nowadays such thinking is clearly out of date.

To understand social behaviour one needs to understand the meaningful setting in which action takes place. As long as the system of meanings is not known to the observer, any society may qualify as loosely structured; when native values and perceptions are not known and when yet outsider observers persist in imposing their own rules of social regularity, all behaviour may easily appear individualistic and a deviation from the rule. The first priority is thus to identify the system of meanings and perceptions that informs social behaviour. In Thailand that system of perceptions is only marginally informed by doctrinal Buddhism, and although Thai social scientists will lend only scant credence to Buddhist meaning in their explanations, some of them still accept the ideas of loose structure and individualism to describe Thai behaviour. This may be so because they take their own non-reflected experience with life in Thai society for granted and thus do not recognize deeper cultural reasons. It may also be that these Thai analysts measure with their familiarity with life in modern western society.

And indeed, when Thailand is directly compared with a western system of formal rules, whether legal or a social science theory, then there is a lot to be said for loose structure and individualism. The flaw of that argument is, of course, that it totally neglects the rules, values, and perceptions that the Thais go by themselves.

The analysis of the symbolic representations led to the identification of two basic classifying principles, *khuna* (moral goodness) and *decha* (amoral power), that appeared to be of great explanatory value in trying to understand observable Thai interaction. The *decha* dimension of perception and behaviour appeared to correspond to public life, governing behaviour vis-à-vis non-intimate distant persons who are primarily perceived as holders of power and hierarchical position. Behaviour in that public world was characterized by presentation, ordered along lines of hierarchy and relative power, equating a person with his status position, and analytically characterized by relative social distance and access to resources. It was also the relatively unstable sector of interaction, characterized by the laws of amoral power, forceful social control, and a short time perspective; the *decha* dimension presented itself as a kind of ordered flux of potential opportunity or loss where expedient considerations reigned supreme. Yet to fully understand its regularities requires more than the rules of power and opportunity, because bonds also needed to be evaluated according to the *bunkhun* and *kreng* feelings involved.

The rules of behaviour in the *khuna* dimension of trust and communality differed starkly from behaviour in the *decha* dimension, social control being more of a moral nature and the bonds between individuals motivated more by obligation and reciprocity than by expediency. This *khuna* area appeared to centre on the mother as the epitome of morality and dependability, and to be of deep psychological importance for the formation of one's individual identity.

To understand behaviour in Thai social space we need to analyse it on a continuum between the poles of *khuna* and *decha*. While this leaves room for elements of individual choice, it certainly does not warrant hypotheses about loose structure. The rules are clearly given in the Thai system of perceptions, and the fact that the modern legal system is often manipulated to personal advantage only proves that it belongs to the sphere of power. That sphere has its own predictable laws, and a short time perspective.

These core classifications also provided the light in which to understand the fascination with power, protection and auspiciousness, both in public life and religious practice, and the perception of modern times. The impersonal and amoral forces that imbue modern times could be understood within the Thai frame of reference; such an understanding made the accommodation with modernity appear as continuity-in-change. I hypothesize a deep-seated satisfaction with presentation as an essential trait of Thai public life. The depth of this satisfaction is demonstrated by the emotion that is invested in presentation. Presentation is therefore more than superficial reality: it is essential reality, and describes the phenomenon in which external appearance is taken to be the heart. It is the manipulation of form as content, or the synergism of these two, in the sense that they are understood and taken as being one and the same thing. In retrospect, it appears that presentation may be a felicitous term to describe public interaction in which a person is equated with his rank, power and status, while the term has less value in depicting interaction with near persons.

The depth of satisfaction with presentation is also explicit in the Thai ethos, its wisdom and survival value. In confrontation with hierarchy and power, right presentation appears to be instrumental in evoking kindness and protection in return. In confrontation with strangers, right manners and a smile seem to smooth interaction and to induce kind and pleasant mutuality. The care for a conflict-free atmosphere is a purpose unto itself that carries over into all types of interaction. A desire for harmony is also at the root of the marked tendency to efface one's private self in most interactions: the overt expression of self is not only a potential threat to social smoothness but is also feared by the individual himself. On the one hand, the dark forces of personal frustration are threatening to the stability and continuity of one's personal existence, while on the other hand they threaten one's social acceptance and successful functioning. This inhibition of individual expression leads to two opposed reactions. First, it leads to attitudes of resignation and submissive acceptance coupled with low self-confidence. (That repressed self, however, may react in a violent manner if provoked or if suppressed too long). Secondly, inhibition of self-expression is congruent with anticipation and consideration of the feelings of others and thus leads to attitudes of kindness and empathy. Both these reactions do not highlight the individual, or individualism; Thai personality should not be seen in isolation but must be defined by the context of the others to whom he relates.

To understand Thai interaction, one should over and above all else understand power as the central axis around which public life revolves. It is power and/or rank that lead to the prestige and social visibility that are the highest social goals. To be big, to be the boss and give orders, to demonstrate social superiority, and to present one's status are the supreme motives for personal fulfilment and achievement. Socially, therefore, the amassing of power is desirable, admired, and respected; it is a means of self-aggrandizement and is a commodity to enjoy. Nowadays, this enjoyment leads to a flagrant materialism, a never quenched thirst for money and obsessive consumerism.

This study in cultural analysis was primarily an attempt to reduce the experience of everyday life to the cognitive reality that informs it. While acknowledging the importance of the structural factors and the awesome impact of modern times, the study concentrated on the analysis, simplification, and typification of the conceptual world of the Thais. Having done this, it may appear to some readers that I have complicated the explanation of everyday life far beyond the simplicity with which it presents itself. Yet, I am convinced that this reduction of a living reality to a few concepts is a gross simplification that has hardly done justice to the subtleties and intricacies of Thai life. Because of the importance of individual variation and motivation, life is far more complicated and confusing than social analysis can clarify. I can, therefore, only hope that this study has succeeded in tracing a few lines through a world of perceptions that inform everyday experience and, further, that those lines are recognizable to the Thais themselves as well as being helpful for the outsider.

NOTES

Chapter 1

1. See his *Handbook for Mankind.* Bangkok: Sublime Life Mission, 1969; for elaboration, see Peter A. Jackson, 1988.

2. For an exhaustive survey of Thai and foreign interpretations of the development of the Thai economy and its social formations, see C. J. Reynolds and Hong Lysa, Marxism in Thai historical studies, *Journal of Asian Studies,* xliii/1 (November 1983).

3. During the Buddhist Lent (*phansa*) of 1966, there were approximately 24,000 temples accommodating 175,500 monks and 87,000 novices. This makes one monk to every thirty-four adult Buddhist males in a total population of thirty-two million. In the same period during 1986, approximately 33,000 temples housed 285,000 monks and 145,000 novices, making one monk to every thirty-five adult Buddhist males in a total population of fifty-five million.

4. Subsequent to the 25 February 1991 military take-over, the then National Peace-Keeping Council accused many of the businessmen-turned-politicians of being 'unusually rich' and confiscated (part of) their assets.

5. From initial electoral success, the fortune of the party rapidly declined; after the elections of 1997, it was left with only one seat in parliament. The loss of trust is probably related to Chamlong's hardheadedness and authoritarian style, and has certainly much to do with the unavoidable expedient decisions of the political game. According to Chamlong, 'Money bested morality' (interview 1955). This realism is supported by the plots of many Thai movies and novels (p.82).

Chapter 2

1. Some Thais, especially those who travel abroad, hold the view that they can invoke the protective blessing of powerful *saksit* images, such as the Emerald Buddha, when they are far away. They may ask for safety or success in an examination and, if their wish is granted, they promise to redeem the vow upon returning to Thailand, preferably at the place of worship of the *singsaksit* concerned.

2. Translated from Sathian Koset, *Muangsawan lae phisang thewada*. Bangkok: Bannakhan, 1972:309.

3. For elaboration of 'the cult of amulets', see S. J. Tambiah, *The Buddhist saints of the forest and the cult of the amulets*. Cambridge: University Press, 1984.

4. In 'village Thailand' this thinking is still demonstrated by the taboos that guide the washing and the drying of clothing. Preferably, feminine clothing should neither touch nor be on the same line as male clothing. Moreover, feminine clothing should never be hung to dry above the head of a male. Similarly, a female stepping over a male is thought to be highly inauspicious for the male and a threat to his potency.

5. It is true, however, that there are female witches who deal with or manifest evil power. There are also some Buddhist 'nuns' (*maechi*), technically in the sexually neutral *samana-phet* category, who practise healing. Further, most spirit mediums, irrespective of whether they mediate between humans and either *saksit* or evil powers, are female.

6. *Pluk phra*: to charge new amulets and Buddha statues with protective *saksit* power.

Chapter 3

1. This idea is a reference to the long-standing school text for the important course in character and disposition, *The Treasure of the Gentleman* (*Sombat khong phudi*).

2. In December 1991, the *Bangkok Post* reported that Thailand is currently the country with the third highest suicide rate in the world.

Chapter 5

1. Suphathana Deechatiwong na Ayutthaya, *Here I am... Beloved Enemy* (*Chan yu ni...satru thirak*, 1977).

Chapter 6

1. Some of the socially critical views of Siburapha are finally available in translation. It is the "other stories" in Siburapha, *Behind the Painting and Other Stories*. Chiang Mai, Silkworm Books, 2000.

2. For a further discussion of social-critical fiction that brings the subject up into the 1990s, see Mulder 1997: ch. 6.

Chapter 8

1. For more recent statistics, see chapter 1, note 3.

2. The school texts consulted adhere to the directives of the Ministry of Education and, in spite of a multitude of publishers, show little variation in their contents.

3. The *naktham* teaching regarding the understanding of the Buddha Dhamma as a religious system is found in the series *The Scrutiny of the Dhamma Explained* (in Thai). Relevant to the observations about meditation is the volume for the *nak-tham ek* course (pp. 93–253). The questions in prior examinations are published, giving a good idea of the stress on memorization rather than on understanding.

4. In Thai, the title is a pun and can also be translated as 'ceremony to insert *saksit* power in amulets (*pluk phra*)'.

5. In Thai, by Chamnong Thongpraseot; he is a well-known Buddhist publicist.

6. For an excellent and penetrating analysis of the thought of Buddhadasa, see Louis Gabaude, *Introduction à l'herméneutique de Buddhadasa Bhikkhu*. Paris: École française d'Extrême-Orient, 1980. See also, Peter A. Jackson, 1988.

7. For a lively analysis of the two sects concerned, see Apinya Fuengfusakul, "Empire of crystal and utopian commune: two types of contemporary Theravada reform in Thailand." In Hans-Dieter Evers, 1993.

Chapter 9

1. These texts have been analyzed in their entirety in Mulder 1997: ch.1.

BIBLIOGRAPHY

Acts on the Administration of the Buddhist Order of Sangha. Bangkok: The Mahamakut Educational Council, 1963.

Adul Wichiencharoen, Social Values in Thailand. *Social Science Review* 1/1:122–70 (1976).

Anon Aphaphirom, *Social Characteristics and Problems of the Thais* (in Thai), 1974.

Boonsanong Punyodyana, Social Structure, Social System, and Two Levels of Analysis: A Thai View. Hans-Dieter Evers (ed.), *op. cit.*, 1969.

Boonsanong Punyodyana, The Changing Status and Future Role of the Chinese in Thailand. M. Rajaretnam and Lim So Jean (eds.), *Trends in Thailand.* Singapore: Singapore University Press, 1973.

Bunsong Chirawat, et al, *Ethics. Book 5* (in Thai). Bangkok: Watthana Phanit, 1991.

Chai-anan Samudvanija and Suchit Bunbongkarn, Thailand. Zakaria Haji Ahmad and Harold Crouch (eds.), *Military-civilian Relations in Southeast Asia.* Singapore: Oxford University Press, 1985.

Chai-anan Samudavanija, State-Identity Creation, State-Building and Civil Society. Craig J. Reynolds (ed.), *National Identity and Its Defenders. Thailand, 1939–1989.* Clayton, Vic.: Monash Papers on Southeast Asia No. 25, 1991.

Charoenkiat Thanasukthaworn, Religion and the Thai Political System. *Social Science Review* 2/2:100–43 (1977).

Chira Sitasuwan et al., Epidemology of Psychiatric Afflictions in Amphoe Bangkok Noi (in Thai). *Journal of the Psychiatric Association of Thailand* 21/1:1–7 (1976).

ETB (Educational Technique Bureau), Department of Education, *Studybook Preparing for the Experience of Life. Book 4,5* (in Thai). Bangkok: Book Development Culture of the Educational Technique Bureau of the Department of Education, 1978.

ETB (Educational Technique Bureau), Department of Education, *Studybook*

Preparing for the Experience of Life. Section People and Evioronment. Section Our Country and its Neighbours (in Thai). Bangkok: Sales Organization of the Khurusapha, 1992, 1991

Embree, John F., Thailand: a 'Loosely Structured' Social System. *American Anthropologist* 52:181–93 (1950).

Evers, Hans-Dieter (ed.), *Loosely Structured Social Systems: Thailand in Comparative Perspective.* New Haven: Yale University, 1969.

Evers, Hans-Dieter (ed.), *Religious Revivalism in Southeast Asia.* Special focus issue of *Sojourn* 8/1 (1993).

Haas, Mary R., *Thai-English Student's Dictionary.* London: Oxford University Press, 1964.

Hanks, L. M., Merit and Power in the Thai Social Order. *American Anthropologist* 64:1247–61 (1962).

Ingram, J. C., *Economic Change in Thailand, 1850–1970.* Stanford: Stanford University Press, 1971.

Jackson, Peter A., *Buddhadasa: a Buddhist Thinker for the Modern World.* Bangkok: The Siam Society, 1988.

Keyes, Charles F., Buddhism and National Integration in Thailand. *Journal of Asian Studies* 30:551–67 (1971).

Khamsing Srinawk, *The Politician and Other Thai Stories.* Kuala Lumpur: Oxford University Press, 1973. Bangkok: Duang Kamol Co., Ltd., 1975.

Kowit Prawanlaphruek (ed.), *Document Introducing the Revised Curriculum of 1990* (in Thai). Bangkok: Educational Technique Bureau, Ministry of Education, 1990.

Meesook, A. et al., Cultures in Collision: An Experience of Thailand. I. Pilowsky (ed.), *Cultures in Collision.* Adelaide: Australian National Association for Mental Health, 1975.

Mulder, Niels, Origin, Development, and Use of the Concept of Loose Structure in the Literature about Thailand. Hans-Dieter Evers (ed.), *op. cit.,* 1969.

Mulder, Niels, *Monks, Merit, and Motivation: Buddhism and National Development in Thailand.* DeKalb: Northern Illinois University, Center for Southeast Asian Studies, 1973.

Mulder, Niels, *Thai Images: The Culture of the Public World.* Chiang Mai: Silkworm Books, 1997.

Mulder, Niels, *Inside Southeast Asia. Religion. Everyday Life. Cultural Change.* Chiang Mai: Silkworm Book, 2000.

Nidhi Ieosiwong, Thailand: Nation and Country in Primary School Texts. In his *The Thai Nation, Thailand, Textbooks and Monuments* (in Thai), 1995.

Pasuk Phongpaichit and Sungsidh Piriyarangsan, *Corruptions and Democracy in Thailand.* Chiang Mai: Silkworm Books, 1997.

Peltier, Anatole-Rogier, *Introduction à la connaissance des luang pho de Thaïlande.* Paris: Publications de l'École française d'Extrême-Orient Vol. CXV, 1977.

Phaibun Chang-rian, *Thai Social Characteristics and Administration* (in Thai), 1973.

Phaithun Khruakeo, *Characteristics of Thai Society* (in Thai), 1969.

Phillips, Herbert P., *Thai Peasant Personality: The Patterning of Interpersonal Behavior in the Village of Bang Chan.* Berkeley and Los Angeles: University of California Press, 1965.

Piker, Steven, Changing Child Rearing Practices in Central Thailand. Steven Piker (ed.), *The Psychological Study of Theravada Societies.* Contributions to Asian Studies 8. Leiden: Brill, 1975.

Piker, Steven and E. Hollis Mentzer, Personality Profiles for Two Central Thai Villages. Steven Piker (ed.), *op. cit.,* 1975.

Police Department, *Yearbook 1976* (in Thai), 1977.

Prizzia, R., King Chulalongkorn and the Reorganization of Thailand's Provincial Administration. R.D. Renard (ed.), *Anuson Walter Vella.* Honolulu: University of Hawaii, 1986.

Puey Ungphakorn, *Best Wishes for Asia.* Bangkok: Klett Thai Publications, 1975.

Reynolds, C. J., Jit Poumisak in Thai History. *Thai Radical Discourse.* Ithaca: Cornell University, Southeast Asian Program, 1987.

Riggs, Fred W., *Thailand: the Modernization of a Bureaucratic Polity.* Honolulu: East-West Center Press, 1966.

Sensenig, Barton, Socialization and Personality in Thailand. Steven Piker (ed.), *op. cit.,* 1975.

Sensenig, Barton, *Self-Concept and Achievement in Northern Thailand.* Ithaca: Cornell University, Ph.D. dissertation, 1977.

Sivaraksa, S., *Siam in Crisis.* Bangkok: Komol Keemthong Foundation, 1980.

Skrobanek, Walter, *Buddhistische Politik in Thailand mit besonderer Berücksichtigung des heterodoxen Messianismus.* Wiesbaden: Franz Steiner Verlag, 1976.

Snit Smuckarn, *The Influence of the Family upon Thai Personality* (in Thai), 1976, a.

Snit Smuckarn, *If You Have Silver, You Are Minor; if You Have Gold, You Are Senior* (in Thai), 1976, b.

Suntaree Komin, *Psychology of the Thai People: Values and Behavioral Patterns.* Bangkok: NIDA Research Center, 1990.

Suphatra Suphap, *Thai Society and Culture* (in Thai), 1975.

Terwiel, B. J., *Monks and Magic: An Analysis of Religious Ceremonies in Central Thailand.* Lund: Studentlitteratur, 1975.

Terwiel, B. J., The Origin and Meaning of the Thai City Pillar. *Journal of the Siam Society* 66/2 (1978).

Thak Chaloemtiarana, *Thailand: The Politics of Despotic Paternalism.* Bangkok: Thai Khadi Institute, 1979.

Thirabutana, Prajuab, *Little Things*. London: Fontana/Collins 1973.

Titaya Suvanajata, Is Thai Social System Loosely Structured? *Social Science Review* 1/1:171–87 (1976).

Udomsilp Srisaengnam, Analysing the Limits. Interview in *Asiaweek* 3/14, 8:50-1 (April 1977).

Weerayudh Wichiarajote, see Sensenig, *op. cit.*, 1975.

INDEX OF NAMES

Terwiel, B. J. 34, 146
Thak Chaloemtiarana 7, 146
Thanin Kraiwichian 79, 100, 106
Thanom Kittikhachon, Marshal 74, 99
Thanom-Praphat, see Thanom
    Kittikhachon
Titaya Suvanajata 44, 45, 62, 146

Udomsilp Srisaengnam 49, 146

Vajiravudh, King (Rama VI) 52, 92, 118

Weerayudh Wichiarajote 45, 57, 146

Zakaria Haji Ahmad 145